T0306014

The shift to omni-channel represents one of the most profound transformations in distribution and to supply chain as a whole. Getting it right will make the difference between winners and losers in the next few years. A must read to navigate these changing waters.

- Ron Kubera, Senior Vice President and General Manager, E2open

The growth in online retailing represents a revolutionary change that is affecting companies of all kinds. And, the development of omni-channel distribution is a key part of this revolution. Myerson's book provides a thorough coverage of what may be one of the most important business developments to hit the business landscape since the Internet.

- Robert J. Trent, Ph.D., Author of *Supply Chain Financial Management*

Paul Myerson neatly breaks down the omni-channel retail supply chain strategy with practical, step-by-step, guidance for companies to consistently satisfy consumer demand and enhance profit margins while navigating frequent regional market hiccups as well as weathering the occasional global disruption, like what we are facing now with the COVID-19 pandemic.

- William J. Bajor, Ph.D., Director, Graduate and Extended Studies, East Stroudsburg University

Myerson's text is a fascinating exploration of omni-channel supply chains that starts with their history and goes on to discuss best omni-channel retail strategies and the future of the omni-channel approach. Reading this book will be time well spent for both marketing and supply chain management students as well as industry practitioners.

- Dr. Mikhail M. Sher, Assistant Professor, Department of Management and Leadership, Leon Hess Business School, Monmouth University

Omni-Channel Retail and the Supply Chain

Omni-Channel Retail and the Supply Chain

Working Together for a Competitive Advantage

Paul Myerson

Routledge
Taylor & Francis Group

A PRODUCTIVITY PRESS BOOK

First published 2021
by Routledge
600 Broken Sound Parkway #300, Boca Raton FL, 33487

and by Routledge
2 Park Square, Milton Park, Abingdon, Oxon, OX14 4RN

Routledge is an imprint of the Taylor & Francis Group, an informa business

ISBN: 9780367641979 (hbk)
ISBN: 9781003123415 (ebk)

Typeset in Minion
by Deanta Global Publishing Services, Chennai, India

Contents

PART II   Traditional vs. Omni-Channel Marketing

Part I

Omni-Channel Retail and the Supply Chain
Working Together for a Competitive Advantage
Introduction

1

Introduction: Where We Are Today

The days of going to the local department store to buy a television, viewing the options available, and making a purchase now seem "quaint". The emergence of the Internet, smartphones, social media, and other technologies has opened a world of new options for consumers (and businesses) to review, research, and buy online with an ever-increasing array of delivery options.

The emergence of e-commerce has resulted in what is commonly known today as "omni-channel" marketing, in which customers engage with companies in a variety of ways, including in a physical store, and online via websites and mobile apps (Figure 1.1). This puts the supply chain "front and center", as consumers are increasingly demanding, and browse, buy, and return goods through various channels and not just in the traditional "brick-and-mortar" way. Accomplishing this with high levels of service, while remaining profitable, requires real-time visibility of inventory across the supply chain and a single view of the consumer as they continuously move from one channel to another.

While this is a boon to consumers, it has made the already complex global supply chain even more challenging to manage.

On top of that, the 2020 COVID-19 pandemic has accelerated this omni-channel retail trend as consumers need even more ways to order and additional options for last-mile delivery such as curbside pickup. COVID-19 has exposed the lack of flexibility and readiness, resulting in shortages of everything from toilet paper and meats to personal protective equipment (PPE) and ventilators due to a variety of capacity and inventory

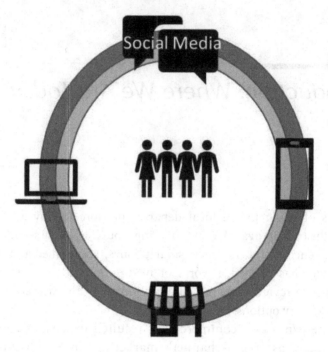

FIGURE 1.1
Omni-channel.

allocation issues. It has been a real-life example of the "bullwhip effect" in action, where variability at the consumer end of the supply chain results in increased variability as you go upstream towards distributors, manufacturers, and suppliers, creating shortages, mis-allocation, and increased costs.

No longer can a manufacturer, distributor, or retailer of consumer products just "fill the pipeline" and wait for orders to come in. Now they must anticipate the various purchase and delivery items, while at the same time minimizing costs. To do this is no easy task, requiring a lean, agile, and responsive supply chain.

Until now, there was no existing "playbook" for organizations to navigate their way through this new world. This book describes the impact of omni-channel marketing on the supply chain and logistics functions and is intended to help management not only meet the needs of today's ever-changing world but also to anticipate what may be required in the future to achieve superior customer service, profitability, and a competitive advantage.

HOW SUPPLY CHAIN STRATEGIES IMPACT E-COMMERCE SUCCESS

E-commerce has emerged as an important part of a company's omni-channel marketing program. Achieving success requires an agile, lean supply chain with a comprehensive strategy on how to get there.

Many e-commerce companies sell a variety of products, and each type of product establishes different strategic needs. For example, functional products require lean and flexible network strategies, while innovative products require more responsive or agile strategies.

Some key factors to consider when employing an e-commerce strategy include:

- Individual product characteristics
- Demand volatility
- Product variety
- Product life cycle length and position
- Criteria for orders, profit margins, and dominant costs – for example, physical vs. marketing
- Quality of information available
- Type of forecast used – qualitative vs. quantitative

In many cases, considering all these factors may result in the need to develop segmented strategies for each supply chain and individual groups of products.

E-commerce has evolved into a combination of retail and industrial product types and industries, as well as Internet technology and devices, the transportation and logistics sectors, and inventory tracking and fulfillment systems (Figure 1.2).

As a result, e-commerce requires strategies that address the following major elements:

The Internet and mobile devices – The platform where sales happen is moving from personal computers to mobile devices such as tablets and smartphones (also referred to as m-commerce).

Omni-channel retailing – This process integrates brick-and-mortar, TV, catalog, social media, e-commerce, and m-commerce channels both for purchases and for returns.

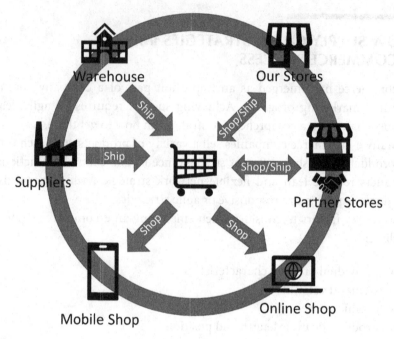

FIGURE 1.2
Omni-channel retail supply chain.

Changing supply chains – In retail, inventory must become more transparent to create efficiencies in new supply chains with direct-to-consumer shipments from online orders, sometimes with returns to stores. Adding to the complexity are ship-to-store and ship-from-store customer orders.

Distribution and fulfillment centers – In the world of e-commerce, companies design and build fulfillment centers to satisfy online orders, which, in many cases, are for a single item. E-commerce orders typically are smaller than those for traditional brick-and-mortar distribution centers, and often require one-day fulfillment.

Automated inventory systems – Beyond the increased current use of radio-frequency identification (RFID), barcode readers, handheld mobile computers, and automated carousels, e-commerce requires companies to plan for the design and implementation of robotic systems in their fulfillment centers and supply chains. These systems can range from the use of automated guide vehicles and robots to the potential future use of air and land drones for delivery.

Online retailing has been growing by an annual average of more than 18 percent globally in recent years, while non-Internet sales are growing by only 1.3 percent annually. As a result, e-commerce is one strategy retailers should not take lightly [Myerson, 2016b].

OMNI-CHANNEL RETAIL AND THE SUPPLY CHAIN: CHALLENGES AHEAD

An omni-channel retail strategy provides an integrated and consistent shopping experience across different channels and devices. Making this strategy a reality requires your supply chain to provide a smooth, positive experience for customers regardless of where and how they interact with your brand.

The omni-channel retail strategy has been driven by the growth of e-commerce and a multi-channel marketing strategy that offers customers multiple ways to buy products (i.e. brick-and-mortar stores, buy at home via the Internet, tablet, smartphone, laptop, or catalogs with home delivery or in-store pick up).

E-commerce sales grew from only 8.0 percent of total U.S. retail sales in 2012 to 16.5 percent in 2019 and accounted for more than half (56.9 percent) of all gains in the retail market in 2019 [Young, 2020]. So, for future success, it is imperative that manufacturers, distributors, and retailers redesign their supply chains to meet growing customer expectations which require real-time visibility of inventory across the supply chain and a single view of the consumer as they go from one channel to another.

Companies must now include omni-channel retail in their supply chain strategies to transform them to be agile and responsive to the changing needs of the consumer, and must build robust data and analytics capabilities.

Some of the challenges ahead that need to be addressed by supply chain executives (covered in more detail in Chapter 9) when dealing with an omni-channel retail strategy include visibility within the supply chain, network design, order fulfillment, pricing, customer service, reverse logistics, and customer engagement.

While these and many other challenges arise from an omni-channel retail strategy, supply chain professionals must rise to the occasion, as it's always better to be part of the solution rather than part of the problem [Myerson, 2018a].

OMNI-CHANNEL MULTIPLIES THE CHALLENGES FOR DISTRIBUTION-CENTRIC SUPPLY CHAINS

Companies today have some big decisions to make about when and how to invest in realigning their supply chains to accommodate an omni-channel pipeline, as, when e-commerce first emerged, most retailers were able to use a small section of an existing distribution center to fulfill online orders. As demand grew, many retailers opened fulfillment centers dedicated to picking and packing individual orders.

To clarify, a distribution center traditionally ships orders in bulk to retailers or wholesalers, while fulfillment centers are designed for packing single orders shipped to an individual end user. On the surface, each has a very different type of operation (and cost structure), as a distribution center typically handles pallet and case quantities and a fulfillment center handles individual piece pick and small parcel orders.

The retail approach today referred to as omni-channel integrates all of a retailer's channels, creating a seamless shopping experience no matter how the shopper is accessing the product.

As part of an omni-channel strategy, some retailers, such as Gap, American Eagle, and now Target, are experimenting with consolidating their distribution and fulfillment centers into one facility, often requiring a new warehouse management system (and material handling systems) intended to better integrate their distribution and fulfillment operations.

In Target's case, at a test facility in Perth Amboy, NJ, their goal is to take their replenishment cycle from days to hours and reduce inventory at stores. This requires sending shipments to stores more frequently and in smaller lots to more precisely meet demand, rather than shipping big cases of products, allowing Target to expand its use of stores to fulfill online orders, with less inventory held at stores, dedicating more room to digital fulfillment.

Before embarking on such a strategy, one must consider the advantages of traditional separated facilities versus combined omni-channel systems.

Some of the advantages of combined facilities include potentially lower operational costs, as fewer facilities generally equate to lower duplication and therefore lower operating costs, shared inventory, and more immediate control and flexibility. This requires a real-time, omni-channel visibility of inventory across the supply chain and a single view of the consumer as they bounce from one channel to another.

On the other hand, there are advantages of having separate facilities such as lower capital costs (since a new shared infrastructure requires significant investment) and having more options when dealing with order fulfillment challenges, as omni-channel facilities handle a lot more stock keeping units (SKUs) than brick-and-mortar retail facilities, meaning there is the potential to run out of space when combined into a traditional distribution center.

Obviously, there's a lot to consider here before making such a huge, long-term strategic decision, but it is one that will have to be made at some point (and sooner rather than later) [Myerson, 2018b].

MANY OPTIONS AVAILABLE

While the Internet and an assortment of technologies give consumers more shopping options, retailers and suppliers also have many options to help with their omni-channel strategy. Depending on your company's size, resources, and goals, there are many ways for companies to meet customer expectations, including keeping it entirely in-house (in combined distribution and fulfillment facilities or separate as previously mentioned), outsourcing processes, or creating a hybrid system.

In-House

While many retailers keep e-commerce fulfillment in-house, some may require a third-party partner to provide omni-channel supply chain technology solutions in order to combine shopping channels with one view of stock. In that way, retailers can make sure that their customers shop the full omni-channel brand and not just one single channel.

Outsource

Others may decide to outsource e-commerce, marketing, electronic data interchange (EDI), fulfillment, and other processes or may determine a hybrid system that works for their needs. This may be a good option for smaller companies with lower costs to get commerce with omni-channel retail.

Hybrid

In the case of a hybrid system, some processes are performed in-house, and others are outsourced, such as EDI and logistics. This helps retailers of all sizes to have a flexible, evolutionary strategy that allows for the movement of key processes to the Web over time without major supply chain disruptions.

INTEGRATED MARKETING AND COMMUNICATION PLANS

When implementing an omni-channel strategy, your marketing plans need to be centralized and integrated across all channels.

If you have different departments managing different channels, there may be multiple voices speaking with prospects and customers, giving too many conflicting messages and overloading them with options. Centralizing and coordinating your marketing efforts is an important infrastructure configuration that needs to be addressed before you start an omni-channel initiative.

Omni-channel retailing principles should also be applied to external and internal organizational communication due to similarities in their nature. Consumers and employees do not want to be forced to use a single communication channel; they want to be able to switch seamlessly and effortlessly between communication channels, without restarting the conversation.

BENEFITS OF OMNI-CHANNEL TO RETAILERS AND THEIR SUPPLY CHAIN

While, like many large retailers, you may already be successful with what you've tried in the past, it takes a different strategy to be successful with omni-channel.

"Omni" means that you must be present on the channels where your customers are, which means that you need to create an omni-channel retail and supply chain strategy that clearly sets goals for what you're trying to accomplish, knowing where your customers and prospects are and determining where your strengths, weaknesses, opportunities, and threats are.

If you are successful in this endeavor, the benefits will be numerous, including increased visibility across the supply chain with optimized inventory, more options for fulfillment to reach more customers, a seamless shopping experience with greater customer service, reduced returns, and more opportunities to engage customers and increase sales.

So, read on to figure out how to leverage your supply chain to achieve a competitive advantage in the digital, omni-channel landscape. The first step is understanding how we got to where we are today, which is the topic of Chapter 2.

2

How We Got Here: From the General Store to Omni-Channel Retail

While the retail industry is undergoing major changes with the advances of e-commerce and omni-channel, it is important to understand the phases throughout its history that have shaped the retail landscape of today.

All one has to do to see how retail has changed over the years is to walk into one's neighborhood supermarket, where one will see a vast assortment of products, giving the consumer seemingly endless choices and an array of technology to make the selection and checkout process smooth and easy.

Large wholesalers have similarly increased the number of choices and the use of technology to speed up the distribution process, as I saw at a large distribution center (DC) of W. W. Grainger, a Fortune 500 industrial supply company. Their DC is modern and automated and can process thousands of orders per day, the majority of which are accurate and complete. Their catalog lists over 400,000 items and customers can purchase over 900,000 items online.

We need to keep in mind that the journey isn't nearly complete in terms of people, process, or technology. In many cases, large retailers, e-tailers, and wholesalers are further ahead as a result of greater resources, but even they can find room for improvement.

While we don't want to "drive forward while looking in the rearview mirror", it sometimes helps to look back before looking ahead.

First, let's get a few definitions out of the way...

RETAIL VS. WHOLESALE

As we know, retail is a critical part of a distribution channel (Figure 2.1), which typically consists of a manufacturer, a distributor or wholesaler, and a retailer.

Retail and Wholesale Defined

A retailer purchases goods or products in large quantities from manufacturers directly or through a wholesaler, and then sells smaller quantities to the consumer for a profit. Retailing can be done in either fixed locations like stores, markets, and door-to-door, or by means of delivery (from a catalog or website).

An e-tailer is a form of retail that exclusively sells goods via electronic transactions on the Internet and is part of the broader category known as e-commerce which encompasses commercial transactions conducted electronically on the Internet.

A wholesaler, on the other hand, is a business that buys large quantities of goods from various producers or vendors, stores them, and resells them to retailers. Wholesalers who carry only non-competing goods or lines are called distributors.

Retailers and wholesalers satisfy their customers' demands through a supply chain.

Retail Classifications and Types

The typical classifications of retail are by type of product, and the major classes are:

• Food products – Includes various food and beverage products.

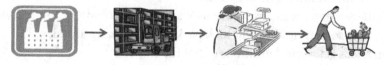

Manufacturer   Wholesaler   Retailer   Customer

FIGURE 2.1
Channels of distribution.

- Hard goods or durable goods – Includes appliances, electronics, furniture, sporting goods, etc. This type of good doesn't wear out quickly and provides utility over time.
- Soft goods or consumables – Includes clothing, apparel, and other fabrics. These goods are consumed after one use or have a limited time period in which to use them.

There are many types of retailers by marketing strategy. The major ones by product line are:

- Department stores – Large stores offering a great assortment of "soft" and "hard" goods. These types of stores typically carry a variety of categories and have a broad assortment. This category includes mass merchandisers such as Walmart and Target, and so-called "category killers" including Home Depot and Bed Bath & Beyond, who dominate one area of merchandise.
- Supermarkets – A self-service store that sells a wide variety of items such as food, toiletries, household products, etc.
- Specialty stores – A smaller store that gives attention to a particular category and provides a high level of service to the customers.
- Discount stores – Stores that offer a wide array of products and services, but compete mainly on price and offer an extensive assortment of merchandise at low prices.
- Convenience stores – Small self-service stores that provide limited amounts of merchandise (food and non-food) at higher than average prices with fast checkout.
- Hypermarkets – Very large self-service stores that provide variety and huge volumes of exclusive merchandise at low margins. The operating cost is comparatively lower than other retail formats. They typically combine a supermarket with a department store (Walmart and Target, for example, have a growing number of stores with these characteristics).
- Warehouse stores – Warehouses that offer low-cost, often high-quantity goods on pallets or shelves. Warehouse "clubs" usually charge a membership fee.
- E-tailers – Stores that sell goods on the Internet. The customer can shop and order through the Internet, and the merchandise is delivered to the 'customer's home.

- Multi-channel – This is the merging of retail operations to enable customer sales through many channels. These channels can include retail ("brick-and-mortar") stores, online stores, mobile stores, mobile app stores, telephone sales, and any other method of selling to a customer. The transactions can include browsing, buying, and returning as well as pre- and post-sale service.
- Omni-channel – A cross-channel strategy that organizations use to improve their user experience and drive better relationships with their audience across points of contact. Rather than working in parallel, communication channels and their supporting resources are designed and orchestrated to cooperate seamlessly.

HISTORY OF RETAIL

As mentioned previously, it's sometimes best to see where we've been before deciding where we want (or need) to go. So, let's look at a brief history of retail below.

Pre-World War II

Prior to 1945, retail was primarily made up of "mom-and-pop" and general stores. The mom-and-pop stores were family-owned and included grocery and hardware stores. General stores offered a wide variety of items.

Retail Growth (1945–1975)

This period saw Woolworth's innovation of taking products from behind the counter and displaying them on the shelves, thus creating the self-service model, where shoppers didn't constantly require an associate's help.

Post-World War II was the era of chain stores such as Sears, J.C. Penney, and Macy's. They expanded from cities into the growing suburbs in large malls and shopping centers. This was also a period for the rapid growth of large supermarket chains such as A&P, Safeway, and Kroger.

Big Box and Category Killers (1975–1990)

During this time, there was rapid growth of mass merchandisers such as Walmart, Kmart, Sears, etc. It was also the beginning of what became known as "category killers", superstores that specialized in one category such as Best Buy, Staples, and Bed Bath & Beyond.

Retail Consolidation (1990–2000)

In this period, there was much industry consolidation as the larger chains such as Walmart, Kohl's, and Home Depot grew bigger and smaller chains and mom-and-pop stores closed. The list of now defunct retailers seems endless, including such names as Caldor, Ames, E.J. Korvette, and Woolworth.

There was also the start and growth of supercenters and warehouse stores which feature "one-stop shopping". This was part of Walmart's successful growth strategy.

As a result, many manufacturers had a shrinking list of retail customers who now had greater negotiating power on price and the supply chain.

The 21st Century (2000–Present)

Consolidation has had a major effect on the merchandising strategies of both shoppers and suppliers. As retailers increase the use of private-label products, there is less leverage available to major brand names. This also gives customers the opportunity for the same or similar quality at a lower price.

Modern technology has even enabled individuals, traditional retailers, and e-commerce businesses like Amazon to sell online.

Mobile commerce, with customers shopping at home, in stores, and on the go, no matter where they are located, is ubiquitous with personalized customer experiences becoming essential. The lines between the online and brick-and-mortar channels are now blurred, with customers demanding options such as buying online and picking up in store (BOPIS). To some degree, shopping is now more of a leisure activity that consumers enjoy.

As a result, omni-channel experiences are what consumers expect, and if you're not meeting their needs you will lose them to your competitors.

In fact, retail e-commerce has grown to over $450 billion/year in 2017 (a 16 percent increase compared with $390.99 billion in 2016) yet is still only 9 percent of total retail sales. However, it continues to grow at a rapid pace (16 percent vs. only 4.4 percent growth for the broader U.S. retail market in 2017). This, to some degree, fills the void left by retail consolidation.

In addition to pure e-tailers, "brick-and-mortar" retailers such as Walmart and Target have a substantial presence on the Internet with online stores morphing into an omni-channel retail experience.

Generation "Y" shoppers have grown up with technology sustaining the Internet's growth as a retail channel.

Some mid-priced stores such as Sears and J.C. Penney have struggled, while discounters, specialty, and luxury stores have done fairly well.

Digital and Physical Experience

The "experience" is changing as well. For example, the Audi City Digital Showroom is a virtual car dealership where customers can customize their car in-store and complete the purchase online at home (or vice-versa). This allows them to combine the best of digital with customer service, and the smaller footprint of the virtual showroom allows dealerships to be located in malls or downtown locations.

Adaptive pricing is already common in certain industries, where prices change based upon variables such as demand, user purchase and search history, time of day, product availability, and location.

UK-based retailer Tesco created a virtual grocery store which allows shoppers to scan QR codes in a subway or airport and have products delivered to their homes after completing the transaction on their phones.

Amazon Locker provides you with a self-service delivery location to pick up and return your Amazon.com packages. Lockers are currently available in a variety of locations throughout the United States. Once your package is delivered to the Amazon locker, 'you'll receive an email notification with a unique pickup code that includes the address and opening times for your selected locker location.

We are also now seeing what are called "flash sales" (see Figure 2.2) by companies such as Groupon who reach shoppers via email and smartphones, with sales at various retailers that are good for only a limited amount of time.

FIGURE 2.2
"Flash sale" example.

Shoppers, using social sites found on their smartphones, find value in browsing social recommendations provided by friends, trend-setters, other shoppers, or celebrities.

Tablets and mobile tools are now part of the in-store experience as well, detailing everything from in-door maps, to checkout, to detailed product information.

Trends such as crowd-sourcing are of increasing impact. An example is a travel app Flightfox where users can submit their travel plans and, for a flat fee, have "experts" compete to provide the winning itinerary including travel information, visa, seat, and city advice.

As shoppers share more personal information, and retailers find ways to access and use these data, the overlap between online and in-store retail will become relatively seamless.

However, it appears likely that retailing will continue, for at least the near future, to be led by large mass merchandisers that have highly efficient supply chain and logistics processes, and specialty retailers that have great selection, customer service, and shopping experience, and e-commerce [www.smyyth.com, 2011].

RETAIL'S VALUE IN THE DISTRIBUTION CHANNEL

As shown in Figure 2.1, retail is the last stage in the supply chain before products or services get to the customer. As such, retail provides a variety of functions that add value for the customer.

Value as a Utility

As both retailers and wholesalers are "intermediaries" and provide a utility or value to the customer, it is useful to first look at the value they provide from a theoretical "utilitarian" perspective. The utilities they provide include:

- Form utility – Performed by the manufacturers (as well as third-party logistics companies or "3PLs" that perform value-added activities such as kitting and display assembly) to make the products useful.
- Time utility – Having products available when needed.
- Place utility – Having items available where people want them.
- Possession utility – Transfer ownership to the customer as easily as possible, including the extension of credit.
- Information utility – Opening two-way flows between parties (i.e. customer and manufacturer).
- Service utility – Providing fast, friendly service during and after the sale and teaching customers how to best use products. This is becoming one of the most important utilities offered by retailers.

Retail (and wholesale, upstream) provides these utilities to one degree or another.

Value as an Activity

In a more practical sense, retailers provide value through a variety of ways, including:

- Assortment – Manufacturers produce a limited number of items whereas supermarkets can carry upwards of 50,000 items. Thus retailers are able to offer a wide assortment of products to consumers at one location.

- Sorting or breaking bulk – Manufacturers can achieve economies of scale in production and transportation costs by shipping in large quantities. When applicable, wholesalers offer in smaller quantities to retailers, and in all cases, retailers offer in smaller quantities to consumers.
- Hold inventory – Retailers hold inventory so that it is readily available to consumers who have limited space in their homes.
- Provide services – Retailers provide value-added services such as credit, displays to test, product demonstrations, and salespeople to answer questions [Levy and Weitz, 2012].

Wholesale also offers value in a similar fashion, albeit upstream, to its retail customers.

All of these activities provide value in the eyes of the customer and help organizations to focus on what adds value and what does not, as we will see below in terms of the "value chain".

Vertical Integration to Add Value

In the supply chain, manufacturing, wholesale, and retail activities are typically accomplished by different organizations. In some instances, there is vertical (backward or forward) integration.

In retail, an example of backward integration occurs where a retailer operates its own distribution centers to supply its stores (fairly common with medium- to large-size retailers). Backward integration also can occur when a retailer has some manufacturing (owned or contracted) or wholesaling activities for private-label items.

A forward integration example would be when a manufacturer operates its own retail stores, such as Nike outlet stores, or a retailer operates a separate return center.

Value Chain

Vertical integration can be an ideal way for a retailer to increase the effectiveness of its "value chain" (the name of a model originated by Michael Porter that shows the value-creating activities of an organization; Figure 2.3) [Porter, 1998].

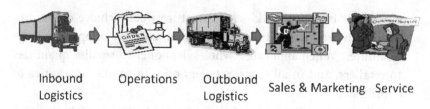

| Inbound Logistics | Operations | Outbound Logistics | Sales & Marketing | Service |

FIGURE 2.3
Primary value chain activities.

Activities That Add Value

In a value chain, each of a firm's internal activities listed below adds incremental value to the final product or service by transforming inputs to outputs (also see Figure 2.3).

- Inbound logistics – Receiving, warehousing, and inventory control of input materials.
- Operations – Transforming inputs to the final product or service to create value.
- Outbound logistics – Actions that get the final product to the customer including warehousing and order fulfillment.
- Marketing and sales – Activities related to buyers purchasing the product, including advertising, pricing, distribution channel selection, etc.
- Service – Activities that maintain and improve a product's value and include customer support, repair and warranty service, etc.

There are also support activities identified by Porter that can add value to an organization which are:

- Procurement – Purchasing raw materials and other inputs that are used in value-creating activities.
- Technology development – Research and development, process automation, etc., which support value chain activities.
- Human resource management – Recruiting, training, development, and compensation of employees.
- Firm infrastructure – Finance, legal, quality, etc.

As we can see, vertical integration as illustrated by the value chain model can be used to increase value and decrease waste in a firm's *entire* value system, including upstream suppliers and downstream buyers. This emphasizes the importance of collaboration among supply chain members, which is critical to managing omni-channel retailing.

Strategies for Tough Times

As it appears that we are in for many years of slow growth and growing competition, many retailers have struggled to come up with strategies to succeed, many of which are good ideas but "piecemeal" efforts to say the least. The various strategies as laid out by Berman and Evans in *Retail Management: A Strategic Approach* [Berman and Evans, 2012] include:

- Re-think existing store formats – In urban areas, Walmart has used a strategy of smaller-format stores. To succeed in this strategy, Walmart will reduce product assortments and maximize their supply chain efficiencies, so stockouts are minimized despite lower in-store inventory levels. They also have a "site-to-store" program which allows customers to order goods online (where Walmart has a much wider product offering), and then have selected goods delivered to a local store for customer pickup.
- Increased use of "pop-up" (or temporary) stores – This is a relatively new phenomenon but has increased in popularity due to high retail vacancy rates and bargain-hunting shoppers. It's not just for holiday shopping, as pop-up stores may also carry manufacturer overstocks, discontinued merchandise, and designer samples.
- Low inventory levels to reduce markdowns – Especially in a bad economy, retailers need to avoid high markdowns. They can do this by looking for special deals, closeouts, etc. Some retailers such as Foot Locker and Champs are expanding their inventory at a slower rate and focus purchases on more popular items.
- Increased promotions using coupons – Coupon distribution and consumer usage are on the rise.
- Shopper discounts based on credit card purchases – Store-branded credit cards are offering discounts/rebates that also tend to increase purchases/visits.
- Begin the holiday season earlier – We've all noticed that Christmas, Thanksgiving, and even Halloween shopping seems to start earlier each year. As retailers order 6+ months ahead anyway, combined with a sluggish economy, holiday sales are starting earlier each year it seems.

- Re-introduce layaway plans – Layaway plans have been around for many years and are making a comeback to both stimulate sales and offer credit to cash-starved shoppers. In this type of plan, a customer pays the product's total cost (usually with a small fee) in installments before being allowed to take the item home.

Now that we've discussed how we've gotten to where we are today, let's consider the subtle and not so subtle differences between multi-channel and omni-channel retailing, each requiring different retail and supply chain strategies.

3

Multi-Channel vs. Omni-Channel

Unless you are a "mom-and-pop" business buying from wholesalers and distributors, you most likely do business today as either a multi-channel or omni-channel retailer.

While both multi- and omni-channel involve selling across multiple physical and digital channels, the main point of differentiation is how the customer experience is (or is not) connected across channels (Figure 3.1).

It can be said that all omni-channel experiences use multiple channels, but not all multi-channel experiences are omni-channel.

MULTI-CHANNEL RETAIL

Multi-channel is typically based on the assumption that customers choose a main way to connect, whether physical stores or a website on the Internet. In many companies, each channel is siloed and managed separately with different teams, budgets, processes, tools, reporting structures, and revenue goals.

In multi-channel retail, stores have their own stock and sell directly to customers, while the website will have its own, separate stock. Items purchased in stores can only be returned in-store, and in many cases, online orders cannot be returned in-store. As a customer, your online interaction with the retailer is completely separated from your offline interaction. In other words, the online and offline channels are treated as separate businesses.

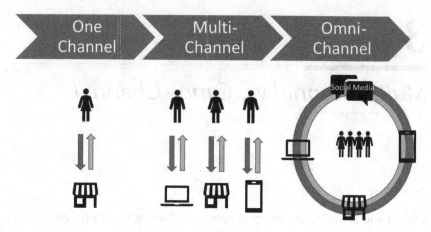

FIGURE 3.1
From brick-and-mortar to omni-channel.

OMNI-CHANNEL RETAIL

On the other hand, in an omni-channel environment, consumers are likely to have multiple touchpoints with a retailer and expect their interactions between each channel be seamless. The idea is that a customer can order what they want, when they want, on whatever device they want, and have it delivered how they want.

A key difference between multi-channel and omni-channel is that omni-channel joins the touchpoints together so that, whatever method or combination of methods the customer chooses in order to make a purchase, the experience is consistent, seamless, and unified for the customer.

Omni-Channel Fulfillment

The fulfillment part of omni-channel can be tricky however, as there are different models within an omni-channel environment, as some companies sell online only, others have brick-and-mortar stores and have added an online channel while still others started off as online-only companies but are adding some form of showroom-only storefront or pop-up store (not to mention Amazon's acquisition of the brick-and-mortar grocery retailer, Whole Foods).

Omni-channel customers buying online may take delivery in different forms from one order to the next (in addition to the traditional visit to a brick-and-mortar retail location). Table 3.1 shows some of the basic online fulfillment options.

Last-Mile Delivery

Furthermore, e-commerce has been creative and innovative in what is known as the "last mile" of delivery to the consumer's home or business, making it much more challenging for traditional retailers. Besides home package last-mile delivery by companies like USPS, FedEx, and UPS, e-commerce businesses like Amazon have been exploring (air and land) drone delivery and lockers in pre-designated, mostly urban, locations available for customer pickup, among other methods.

Traditional last-mile delivery involves many challenges including cost minimization, transparency, and efficiency. These challenges, along with the growth of e-commerce, are forcing brick-and-mortar retailers to become more creative.

To meet this challenge, some large retailers such as Walmart and Best Buy are even using their brick-and-mortar stores as distribution centers.

TABLE 3.1

Omni-Channel Online Fulfillment Options

Omni-Channel Order Placement	Method for Order Fulfillment
Buy online, ship to home or office	DC ships order directly to customer
Buy online, ship to store	DC ships order to brick-and-mortar store for customer pickup
Buy online, pickup in-store (often same day)	Order picked and ready in-store for customer pickup
Buy online, ship from store	Store picks and ships order to customer's home or office
Buy online, drop ship from vendor	Vendor ships order to customer's home or office
Buy online and pickup at locker (which is located close to customers in stores, buildings, etc.)	DC ships order to locker at pre-designated location
Select from showroom-only storefront and scan QR code to buy online	DC ships order to customer's home or customer picks up at storefront

Basically, store employees pick items from the store shelves and backrooms to fulfill online orders and either drop them into waiting FedEx or UPS trucks or, in some cases, deliver the orders themselves which is being tested in a few Walmart stores.

Stores can stand to cut a significant amount of costs by having employees deliver from stores, as the "last-mile" costs for delivery are a significant part of fulfillment costs. Employee delivery is potentially even better than having a third party such as UPS or even Uber drivers do it (also being tested) as they would have to drive to the store, whereas the employee is already there. Furthermore, in the case of Walmart, two-thirds of the U.S. population live within 5 miles of a Walmart.

Some other benefits of store last-mile delivery include switching online orders to locations with the most inventory of a selected item, thereby reducing the need for discounts, and fulfilling orders for items that are out of stock at e-commerce fulfillment centers (which happens 2–4 percent of the time at Best Buy for example).

This concept is even more important as Amazon continues to expand its network of fulfillment centers to bring them closer to customers. By enabling store delivery, traditional retailers feel they can better compete with Amazon's fulfillment network of 100+ distribution centers by utilizing their hundreds or even thousands of brick-and-mortar locations as DCs.

A Unified Approach

To offer a unified approach, omni-channel initiatives often are driven through digital transformation projects. Most take a gradual approach, starting with existing systems and integrating them (e.g. separate POS, ERP, and WMS systems). While there are a number of companies offering new solutions that can help a retailer move towards omni-channel, there are only a few technology solutions that cover multiple significant areas of an omni-channel business (that will surely change over time).

There are major process and cultural changes required as well, beyond the supply chain challenges that we will cover later in this book, for example when a brick-and-mortar retailer decides to become omni-channel, there may be an "us vs. them" attitude from in-store personnel as the customer may actually shop using a combination of in-store, online, on the telephone, or live chat conversation. If your system can track and unify all of these interactions and you can give the in-store staff credit and commission for the sale (on big-ticket items at least), you will probably be more successful in the long run. These process and technology changes can be costly and complex.

If the move to omni-channel is adequately supported by a digital platform along with organizational and cultural changes that result in collaboration and communication, then a company can act as a unified organization with all employees working together to give customers what they are looking for along their digital shopping journeys.

It seems that there are very few retailers who have fully embraced omni-channel, but consumers will start to drive brands through their desires and behaviors to invest in the technology and cultural change that are required. By sticking with multi-channel, companies will drive away customers who want to design their own journey towards the competition.

THE OMNI-CHANNEL EXPERIENCE VARIES AS SHOWN BY SOME EXAMPLES

As mentioned, the multi-channel experience is what most businesses invest in today through websites, blogs, Facebook, and Twitter to engage and connect with customers. However, a seamless experience and consistent messaging are lacking across these channels.

An omni-channel experience, on the other hand, accounts for each platform and device a customer will use to interact with the company. That knowledge is then used to deliver to them an integrated experience with an integrated supply chain to support it. Companies using this technique align their messaging, goals, objectives, design, and processes across each channel and device.

To truly deliver an omni-channel experience for your customers, it is necessary to start with a strategic plan to build an aligned experience across multiple platforms that considers all internal and external stakeholders, which we will discuss later in the book.

An omni-channel strategy is about developing the intelligence needed to know the right resources to use to create a satisfying yet profitable consumer experience, as:

- Seventy-nine percent of consumers spend upwards of 50 percent of their shopping time researching products online.
- Eighty-two percent of consumers substitute and switch brands due to an out-of-stock product.
- Fifty-nine percent of consumers will try a new brand to get better customer service.

Access and Sharing of Information Is Key

Ultimately, the consistency and availability of information across offline and online channels, as well as supply chain efficiency, determine the consumer experience.

Leading retailers use consumer intelligence to adjust marketing and merchandising strategies to align with real-time product preferences and more tactically to help make better decisions regarding their marketing mix and promotional calendars.

Business intelligence (BI) and related technology can help to align operations and optimize the sharing of insights across the buyer journey by enabling retailers to collect, centralize, and publish data across channels in real time. This allows retail marketers to not only align product information, branding, and messaging across all channels but also to transform the entire organization to align sales, customer service, supply chain, and planning and forecasting efforts with the needs of consumers.

Other things that are important to a successful omni-channel strategy include the ability to:

- Share order management information across channels, thereby increasing visibility for both the customer and employees throughout the entire order process, from the transaction through fulfillment.
- Integrate consumer data and insights into business operations plans, including supply, pricing, and promotions.
- Establish consumer data collection standards for all channels to enable a holistic, actionable view of consumers.

Integrated business-wide involvement in the consumer experience is the real goal of any successful omni-channel strategy [Robinson, 2014].

As this is a relatively new concept, and somewhat unique to each company, it's best at this point to look at some successful examples of omni-channel brands (mostly retailers, but in some cases manufacturers and distributors who sell direct to consumers via e-commerce and/or "brick-and-mortar").

Example #1: Crate & Barrel

As shoppers tend to switch from the e-commerce website to smartphone to tablet when conducting research and completing purchases, the Crate & Barrel app saves their e-commerce shopping cart so they can access their information across multiple mobile devices and browsers, offering a seamless shopping process.

Crate & Barrel provides a seamless customer experience to shoppers using its wedding and gift registry, where customers can create and monitor their registries online and in the store as well as with an app that lets them manage their registry from their mobile devices as well.

The app allows users to create and edit their registry, scan barcodes in the stores to add items, and see purchases made in real time.

Example #2: Oasis

UK fashion retailer Oasis has an e-commerce site, a mobile app, and brick-and-mortar locations that combine channels to give people a holistic shopping experience.

In-store associates have iPads to give shoppers information on product availability and check out customers from anywhere in the store, and if an item isn't in-stock, they can place e-commerce orders on the spot.

Online customers can use Oasis' "Seek & Send" service where the retailer searches its stores for the product and ships it to the shopper, sending an email to help them track their goods.

Besides letting people return items via mail or return them to any Oasis branch, they also have a service that lets shoppers return purchases through a network over 5,500 drop-off points in local stores, including convenience stores and grocery stores.

Example #3: Starbucks

The Starbucks rewards app provides an integrated user experience across all channels where customers have the option of checking and reloading their Starbucks card balance through their phone, website, or at the store. Balance, reward updates, or profile changes are updated in real time, across all channels, no matter where they are or what device they're using.

Customers can pay with their rewards card or their phone, and the balance will automatically be updated online and in the app.

Example #4: Sephora

Fashion retailer Sephora's "My Beauty Bag" program makes it easy for its loyal customers to manage their products and purchase history from any mobile device.

Customers can use their Beauty Bag on their mobile or on their computer to view and track their purchases and rewards as well as to add items to their shopping list, view their buying history, save items for future purchases, and re-order items.

Example #5: Chipotle

Chipotle Mexican Grill utilizes multiple channels to enable customers to place orders online or with a mobile app for dine-in or pickup at the nearest Chipotle location.

Users can also track past orders and save their favorites for quicker ordering in the future.

Ultimately, a successful retail omni-channel strategy should determine the key tasks or actions that customers perform throughout the shopping experience, and then let them accomplish those tasks across multiple channels. Omni-channel retailing isn't just about selling across multiple channels, it's also about letting the customer do whatever they need to do throughout their entire shopping journey with any device or platform they're on [Trout, 2017].

Before looking at potential omni-channel supply chain strategies and tactics later in the book, it is important to first understand the marketing strategies that create omni-channel demand.

Part II

Traditional vs.
Omni-Channel Marketing

4

Marketing 101

DEFINITIONS AND OVERVIEW OF MARKETING

While this is surely not a marketing book, to better understand how the supply chain can support an omni-channel, or any retail strategy, it is important to first understand the basics of marketing.

From a macro view, marketing is the activity, set of instructions, and processes for creating, communicating, delivering, and exchanging offerings that have value for customers, clients, partners, and society at large.

In business terms, marketing is a critical process responsible for identifying, anticipating, and satisfying customer requirements profitably with the goal of attracting new customers by promising and delivering superior value and satisfaction.

Originally, marketing was about making the sale, whereas today it is more about identifying and satisfying customer needs.

Advertising, on the other hand, is a process of announcing or praising a product or service in some public medium of communication in order to induce people to buy or use it.

Finally, what is commonly referred to as "branding" is a trademark or distinctive name identifying a product or a manufacturer (e.g. a popular brand of soap).

The Marketing Process and the Steps Involved

The marketing process itself involves:

- Understanding the marketplace and customer needs and wants.
- Designing a customer-driven marketing strategy.

- Constructing an integrated marketing program that delivers superior value.
- Building profitable relationships and creating customer delight.
- Capturing value from customers to create profits and customer quality.

First, we need to identify wants and needs. In general, need is the state of perceived deprivation of physical, social, and individual needs as identified by:

- Physical needs – Food, clothing, shelter, safety.
- Social needs – Belonging, affection.
- Individual needs – Learning, knowledge, self-expression.
- Want – Form that a human need takes, as shaped by culture and individual personality.

Ultimately, "wants" plus buying power equal demand.
  Needs and wants are fulfilled through a specific marketing offering that includes:

- Products – People, places, organizations, information, and ideas.
- Services – Activities or benefits offered for sale that are intangible and do not result in ownership.
- Experiences – Consumers using the offering.

Dependent on the product's perceived performance relative to a buyer's expectations, care must be taken when setting expectations. If performance is lower than expectations, satisfaction is low, and if performance is higher than expectations, satisfaction is high. Customer satisfaction often leads to consumer loyalty, so some firms seek to "delight" customers by exceeding expectations.

Marketing Management: Strategy, the Value Proposition, and Marketing Mix

Now that marketing has been defined, it is important to understand marketing "management", which is the art and science of choosing target markets and building profitable relationships with them, and requires that consumers and the marketplace be fully understood. The aim of marketing management is to find, attract, keep, and grow customers by creating, delivering, and communicating superior value.

Marketing managers must consider the following to ensure a successful marketing strategy:

- What customers will we serve, and what is our target market?
- How can we best serve these customers, and what is our value proposition?

The Value Proposition

The value proposition is the set of benefits or values a company promises to deliver to consumers to satisfy their needs. Value propositions dictate how firms will differentiate and position their brands in the marketplace.

The marketing concept is a marketing management philosophy that holds that achieving organizational goals depends on knowing the needs and wants of target markets and delivering the desired satisfaction better than competitors.

Customer-perceived value is the customer's evaluation of the difference between the benefits and costs of a marketing offer relative to those of competing offers. Perceptions may be subjective, and consumers often do not objectively judge values and costs. Therefore, customer value = perceived benefits – perceived sacrifice.

Marketing Mix

The marketing mix is the set of controllable, tactical marketing tools that the firm blends to produce the response it wants in the target market as identified by the 4Ps of marketing (Figure 4.1):

- **Product:** To determine what you should be selling, you need to understand your target customer's needs and tailor your product to meet those needs. The more you can fulfill your customers' expectations, the better the chance that they will buy from you.

    This includes variety, features, brand name, quality, design, packaging, and services.

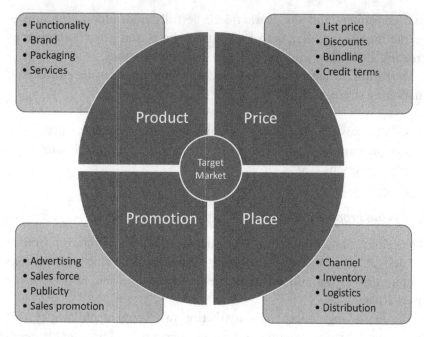

FIGURE 4.1
4Ps of marketing – the marketing mix.

- **Price:** The price that you charge will influence sales volume and the amount sold. Pricing too low may make it look like the product is of lower quality with minimal or no profit, and pricing too high may result in customers buying fewer items in smaller quantities.

  List price, discounts, allowances, payment period, and credit terms are all factors in pricing.

- **Promotion:** For people to buy your product, they need to have an awareness and positive impression of it to help be convinced that they need or want it.

  This includes advertising, sales promotion, public relations, and personal selling.

- **Place:** This refers to both where you are going to sell your product and how you are going to distribute it.

  Consideration must be given to distribution channels, coverage, logistics, locations, transportation, assortments, and inventory.

MARKETING TECHNIQUES TO UNDERSTAND
THE MARKETPLACE AND CUSTOMER NEEDS

A concept known as segmentation is the process of dividing a market into distinct groups of buyers with different needs, characteristics, or behaviors who might require separate products or marketing programs.

Key segmenting variables are geographic, demographic, psychographic, and behavioral.

Different segments desire different benefits from products, and it is best to use multivariable segmentation bases to identify smaller, better-defined target groups

By segmenting, we can meet consumer needs more precisely, increase profits, segment leadership, retain customers, and focus marketing communications.

We need to evaluate market segments' size and growth by:

- Analyzing current segment sales, growth rates, and expected profitability.
- Evaluating segment structural attractiveness by considering competition, existence of substitute products, and the power of buyers and suppliers.
- Determining company objectives and resources by examining the company skills and resources needed to succeed in that segment.
- Offering superior value and gaining advantages over competitors.

Targeting Segments

Once potential segments have been identified, the next step is targeting, which involves evaluating each market segment's attractiveness and selecting one or more segments to enter.

Specifically, market targeting involves:

- Evaluating marketing segments.
- Segmenting size, segment structural attractiveness, and company objectives and resources are considered.
- Selecting identified target market segments.

- Considering alternatives which can range from undifferentiated marketing to micromarketing.
- Being socially responsible.

Differentiation and Positioning

Finally, a differentiation strategy is the act of creating superior customer value by differentiating the market offering, and positioning involves arranging for a product to occupy a clear, distinctive, and desirable place relative to competing products in the minds of target consumers.

A product's position is the way the product is defined by consumers on important attributes, which is, the place the product occupies in consumers' minds relative to competing products.

Perceptual positioning maps can help define a brand's position relative to competitors.

Identifying possible value differences and competitive advantages is key to winning target customers; to accomplish this, it is necessary to understand their needs better than competitors do and to deliver more value.

Competitive advantage is the extent to which a company can position itself as providing superior value and is achieved via differentiation.

Marketing isn't done in a vacuum, as it is integrated with all of the other functions of your business such as:

Research and development (R&D) – Needs to focus on developing products that meet the needs of clients.

Manufacturing, operations, and supply chain – Must be able to meet the demand created for your product at the level of quality promised to your customers.

Human resources strategy – Needs to focus on hiring and training people to sell your product.

Finance – Needs to provide input on the pricing of your product.

Legal – Needs to assess implications of various marketing techniques that you may use.

Environmental – Will want to consider possible packaging of your product to ensure that it has a low impact on the environment.

MARKETING STRATEGY PROCESS

The strategic planning process involves establishing an organizational mission and formulating goals, corporate strategy, marketing objectives, marketing strategy, and a marketing plan (see Figure 4.2).

The general benefits of strategic planning are that it:

- Provides the basis for internal communication among employees.
- Defines the assignment of responsibilities and tasks and sets the schedules for implementation.
- Presents objectives and specifies resource allocations.
- Helps in monitoring and evaluating the performance of the marketing strategy.

Marketing Strategy Development

A marketing strategy requires careful customer analysis. To be successful, firms must engage in market segmentation, targeting, differentiation, and positioning, previously discussed.

To be clear, a marketing strategy is a plan of action for identifying and analyzing a target market and developing a marketing mix to meet

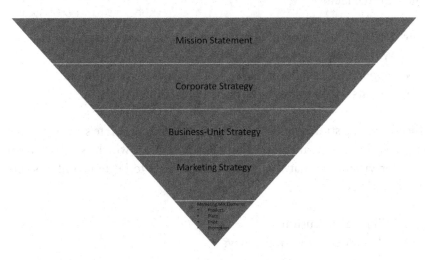

FIGURE 4.2
Levels of strategic planning.

the needs of that market, while a marketing plan is a written document that specifies the activities to be performed to implement and control an organization's marketing activities.

When developing a marketing strategy, it is important to understand your company's core competencies, which are things your firm does extremely well (i.e. strengths), which sometimes give it an advantage over its competition. These include financial and human resources, reputation, good will, and brand names.

Next, you must identify market opportunities, which are a combination of circumstances and timing that permits an organization to reach a target market.

Core competencies are then matched to opportunities while considering strategic windows available, which are temporary periods of optimal fit between the key requirements of a market and the particular capabilities of a firm.

The goal of the marketing strategy is to establish a long-term competitive advantage which is the result of a company's matching a core competency (superior skill or resources) to opportunities in the marketplace in terms of manufacturing, technical, and/or marketing skills.

It is important to do an assessment of the organization's strengths, weaknesses, opportunities, and threats (SWOT) to fully consider internal and external factors.

- Strengths – Competitive advantages or core competencies.
- Weaknesses – Limitations on competitive capability.
- Opportunities – Favorable conditions in the environment.
- Threats – Conditions or barriers to reaching objectives.

The marketing strategy must be aligned with the corporate strategy which is driven by the organization's mission statement, which is a long-term view, or vision, of what the organization wants to become and answers two questions:

1. Who are our customers?
2. What is our core competency?

From that, a marketing objective can be developed, which is a statement of what is to be accomplished through marketing activities to match strengths to opportunities, or to provide for the conversion of weaknesses to strengths. It should be stated in clear, simple terms, be accurately measurable, specify a time frame for accomplishment, and be consistent with business-unit and corporate strategy.

MARKET PROGRAM DEVELOPMENT

After the development of a marketing strategy, it is time to develop an integrated marketing program that will deliver the planned value to targeted customers. The marketing program details how you will put your strategy into action using the marketing mix tools (i.e. 4Ps) to communicate and deliver the intended value to targeted customers.

It will set marketing budgets and deadlines and describe how you're going to reach your target customers, whether through advertising, online through your website or social media, offline by networking and attending trade shows, through direct marketing, etc.

Timing these activities to fit customer buying cycles will help to maximize revenue.

Finally, progress should be regularly measured and reviewed to determine what's working and what isn't, setting new targets as the market changes.

Understanding the marketplace and customer needs, designing marketing strategy, and constructing a marketing program lead to perhaps the most important step of all, which is connecting with customers and profitably managing those relationships.

CREATING AND MANAGING CUSTOMER RELATIONSHIPS

Customer relationship management (CRM), a very important concept in marketing today, is both a strategy and a system for managing an organization's relationships and interactions with customers and potential customers, used to deliver customer value and satisfaction. It uses data analysis about customers' history with a company to improve business relationships with customers, specifically focusing on customer retention and ultimately driving sales growth.

A CRM system is a tool that is used for contact management, sales management, productivity, and beyond and helps companies stay connected with customers, streamline processes, and improve profitability.

CRM's Different Meanings

While the concept of customer relationship management started in the early 1970s, when customer satisfaction was evaluated using annual surveys or by face-to-face interactions, the first CRM software product was introduced by Siebel Systems in 1993. They were eventually improved by integration with enterprise resource planning functions, and shipping and marketing capabilities, and then later enhanced with mobile apps.

Today, there are three different meanings of CRM:

1. As a technology: CRM is a technology product or system that documents, reports, and analyzes interactions between the company and users.
2. As a strategy: It is a business philosophy about managing relationships with actual and potential customers.
3. As a process: It is a system that a business uses to manage relationships with actual and potential customers.

The Benefits and Advantages of CRM

Generally speaking, CRM offers many benefits and advantages to an organization, including:

Enhanced contact management – Every touchpoint with prospects and clients (i.e. calls, questions, negotiations, and other touchpoints) is recorded and accessible to the sales, marketing, supply chain, operations, and customer service teams with a centralized contact management system.

Cross-team collaboration – A CRM system enables people from different parts of a business to work together, such as when a sales team collaborates with a product team to generate quotes, and when details from a lead from a marketing campaign enable a salesperson to have a more customized conversation with a prospect.

Increased productivity – Reduce administrative tasks like follow-up emails which can be auto-generated, enabling management to easily access recent details of a customer meeting, and customer service administrators learning about the background of a customer while simultaneously being on a call with the customer.

Empowered sales management – CRM gives sales managers data to analyze customer relationships, track sales activity and pipeline, get help when needed, and provide teams with real-time updates.

Integrated sales forecasting – Access to data from a CRM can make it easier for sales managers to make accurate forecasts using detailed historical data, and to use predictive analytics from big data to anticipate future customer demand.

Reliable reporting – Enables current review of a company's sales pipeline to spot potential issues.

Reports can also improve productivity by creating pivot tables in spreadsheets instead of manually pulling data together from various sources.

Improved sales metrics – Focus on the leads that are most important with insights into lead conversion effectiveness and help with upselling and cross-selling opportunities from existing customers.

Increased customer satisfaction and retention – Access to customers' interactions makes it easier to anticipate potential issues and successfully deal with complaints, creating a more positive "one-stop" service experience for customers, rather than having to explain their issues multiple times.

Better marketing ROI – Continuous tracking helps businesses to see which marketing activities are most effective with their clients to see what type of marketing works for each type of customer, so as to increase ROI.

Enhanced products and services – CRM systems combine information from a variety of sources, giving insight into customer feelings and opinions so as to improve offerings and to catch problems early [salesforce.com, 2018].

How Do Different Business Functions Benefit from Using CRM?

While CRM has traditionally been used as a sales and marketing tool, some of the biggest benefits can come in other areas, such as customer service, human resources, supply chain, and partner management.

Sales – Sales teams can use CRM to gain a better understanding of their sales pipeline.

Managers have access to information regarding the progress of individual team members in achieving their sales targets, and can see how well sales teams, products, and campaigns are performing as well.

Sales representatives can benefit from reduced administration, a better understanding of their clients, and spending more time selling and less time entering data.

Marketing – Marketing teams can use CRM for more accurate forecasts and to gain more visibility on sales opportunities, giving them a better understanding of the sales pipeline, and to include customers' public social media activity and preferences.

Customer service – Customer service teams can monitor information across channels, such as when a customer issue arises on social media, for example, which can then be resolved on another channel such as email, chat, or a phone call.

Supply chain and logistics – Procurement can manage supplier relationships better by tracking meetings, notes, and follow-ups to manage their entire supply chain more effectively.

Human resources – HR can use CRM to reduce the recruitment cycle and track employee performance.

This can include speeding up the on-boarding process, automating the process of managing candidates, analyzing resourcing needs and identifying skills gaps, and supporting staff retention targets.

In all, a CRM system lets you manage various streams of information across channels and gives sales, service, marketing, supply chain, logistics, and operations an integrated view of the business.

The emergence of the digital age has radically changed marketing in a variety of ways, which is the topic of our next chapter.

5

Omni-Channel Marketing: The Internet and Emergence of E-Commerce and Its Impact on Traditional Marketing

In its most basic meaning, marketing is about creating, communicating, delivering, and exchanging offerings that have value for customers, clients, partners, and society.

For the most part, marketing had changed very little over the centuries until the advent of radio, television, and billboard marketing which made it possible to reach far more people than before.

More recently, the Internet and mobile technology have changed marketing even more radically, with access to exponentially more people with more information to digest, and new tools and techniques to predict buying patterns and customer needs.

Companies today need to tailor their strategies to reach their customers, as a large marketing budget isn't enough to take advantage of multiple marketing channels.

Marketing today is truly omni-channel as companies need to provide a seamless experience, regardless of the channel or device, towards a more personalized, individual communication with consumers, through the various channels and many devices they use.

Consumers can now engage with a company in a physical store, on an online website, mobile app, catalog, or via social media using a phone, on their mobile smartphone, a tablet, a laptop, or a desktop computer. It is critical that the consumer's experience is consistent and complementary.

This involves viewing the experience through the eyes of your customer, integrating the customer experience across all channels so that it is seamless, integrated, and consistent, as customers may start in one channel and move to another as they progress to a resolution.

THE GROWTH OF DIGITAL AND MOBILE TECHNOLOGY

Today, 42 percent of the world's population are online and 58 percent of all American adults own smartphones. In the United States alone, people now spend more time with digital media (5¼ hours) than viewing traditional TV (4½ hours) each day.

Digital and social media marketing uses tools such as websites, social media, mobile ads, apps, online video, email, blogs, etc., to reach consumers via their computers, smartphones, tablets, and other digital devices for promotion, shopping, and assistance (Figure 5.1) [Armstrong and Kotler, 2017].

FIGURE 5.1
E-commerce marketing.

Social Media Marketing (SMM)

Social media marketing (SMM) involves creating and sharing content on social media applications such as Facebook, Twitter, Google+, LinkedIn, YouTube, Instagram, Pinterest, or other social media sites to reach your planned marketing and branding goals. SMM utilizes "real-time" marketing which is a strategy focused on current, relevant trends and immediate feedback from customers.

Social media marketing includes activities such as creating text and image updates, videos, and other content to increase audience engagement, in addition to paid social media advertising.

When creating social media marketing campaigns, you should think about your company's strategic goals before defining your marketing goals.

When defining your social media marketing goals, you should ask questions such as what you are hoping to achieve through social media marketing, who your target audience is, how they use social media, and what message you are trying to send to your audience.

Your business type will also drive your social media marketing strategy; in general, it can help to:

- Increase website traffic.
- Build conversions.
- Raise brand awareness.
- Create brand identity and brand association.
- Improve communication and interaction with targeted audiences.

Social Media Concepts

To be successful in social media marketing you should consider the following ideas:

Social media content planning – Use keyword and competitive research to see what others are doing, which can help you come up with content ideas for your target audience.

Great social content – Post information that your target customers will find helpful and interesting including social media images, videos, infographics, how-to guides, etc.

A consistent brand image – Social media helps your business to place its brand image on a variety of unique social media platforms, while maintaining your business's core identity throughout.

Social media for content promotion – Used to share your website and blog content with readers to build a loyal following. It's an efficient way to combine content marketing and social media marketing.

Sharing curated links – Social media for marketing presents an opportunity to link to outside articles. Curating and linking to other sources can improve trust and reliability and even get some links in return.

Tracking competitors – Competitors can provide valuable data for keyword research and other social media marketing insight, for example, if they are successfully using a particular social media marketing channel or technique maybe consider using it as well.

Measuring success with analytics – You need to track data to see how successful your social media marketing strategies are. Tools such as Google Analytics can be used to measure your social media marketing techniques and to see which strategies are working and which are not. Also use the analytics tools within each social platform to determine which social content is giving the "biggest bang for the buck".

Social media crisis management – There is always a risk for things to go wrong for brands on social media, so having a risk management strategy for handling this is critical.

Social Media Platforms

There is an ever-growing list of social media marketing sites, with each requiring different approaches. The current list includes:

Facebook – An online social media and social networking service. The visual presentation is an important part of the Facebook experience as people go there to catch up and chat with friends. It is important that your tone is light and friendly.

Pinterest – A very fast-growing platform with primarily a female audience where people pin photos into collections called boards, which serve as big catalogs of objects and basically changes Web pages into the objects that are embedded in them. As Pinterest is an image-oriented platform it is best used for retail but can be used by any type of business for social media purposes or advertising. Businesses can showcase their products and develop brand personality "pinboards".

Twitter – An online news and social networking service on which users post and interact with messages known as "tweets".

Tweet about specials, discounts, and news. Retweet when a customer has something nice to say about you, and answer people's questions when possible. Interact as much as possible to build your following.

LinkedIn – A professional social media marketing site which is, in effect, a business networking and employment-oriented service. Forming a LinkedIn "Group" is a great way to have a professional dialogue with people in similar industries and to share content.

Recommendations make your business appear more credible for new customers. Also, providing answers to questions helps you to become a thought leader and gain trust.

YouTube – A website for creating and sharing video content, which can also be a powerful social media marketing tool. A great strategy is to use it to create useful, instructive "how-to" videos, as not many videos go "viral".

Reddit – A social news aggregation, web content rating, and discussion website, which is great for sharing content. The Reddit community tends to be young, geeky, liberal, and Internet-obsessed. So, with that in mind, targeting them can increase traffic to your site.

Social media in marketing can not only improve site traffic and help you reach more customers, it can also help you to gain knowledge of your target audiences [wordstream.com, 2018].

Mobile Marketing (MM)

Mobile marketing (MM) is a multi-channel online marketing technique focused on reaching a targeted audience with ads via their smartphone, tablets, or any other related devices through websites, email, text, social media, or mobile applications. It gives actual or potential customers with smartphones personalized, time- and location-sensitive information so that they can get what they need exactly when they need it, keeping in mind that up to 40 percent of users' Internet time is spent on mobile devices

Mobile Marketing Strategies

Some mobile marketing strategies include:

App-based marketing – This is mobile advertising involving mobile apps, where services like Google AdMob help advertisers create mobile ads that appear within third-party mobile apps.

Facebook also allows advertisers to create ads that are integrated into their mobile app. Known as mobile promoted post ads, they integrate seamlessly with Facebook's News Feed.

In-game mobile marketing – In-game mobile marketing are mobile ads that appear within mobile games and can appear as banner pop-ups, full-page image ads, or video ads between loading screens.

QR codes – Two-dimensional barcodes that are scanned by users, who are then taken to a specific webpage linked to the QR code. QR codes can be integrated into just about any type of printed material, including:

- Conference/event displays
- Print advertisements
- Business cards
- Brochures, posters, and flyers
- Postcards and mailers

Location-based marketing – Ads that appear on mobile devices based upon a user's location relative to a specific area or business.

Mobile search ads – Google search ads built for mobile devices, which may have extra add-on extensions like click-to-call or maps.

Mobile image ads – Ads that are designed specifically to appear on mobile devices.

Short message service (SMS) aka texting – SMS marketing involves sending text offers to users' cell phones. Not used a lot and can be considered a bit intrusive.

Google AdWords – An online advertising service developed by Google, where advertisers pay to display brief advertisements, service offerings, product listings, and video content within the Google ad network to web users. Mobile search ads with Google also let you take advantage of their mobile ad extensions and mobile marketing tips.

Be clear and concise – Cluttered and crowded ads on mobile devices will just cause users to ignore them as they tend to have small screens.

Optimize for local – Optimize for local mobile marketing to make sure you are aligning with users' queries as one in three mobile searches have local intent.

Consider your audience – The type of audience you're aiming for should direct the kind of mobile ads you use (i.e. if they are gamers, maybe use in-game ads; if they are young and tech-savvy, try mobile Facebook promoted posts, etc.).

Experiment with different strategies – Test out different ad extensions with your AdWords-enhanced campaigns such as the Google Offers ad extension (or the click-to-call extension) and see how well they work for you.

Benchmark your results – You need to track the results of what you are testing to see what works. One way is through the AdWords Grader which can show you how your mobile pay-per-click ads are performing, for example [Marrs, 2017].

HOW THE DIGITAL AGE HAS CHANGED MARKETING

There is no doubt that the digital age has forever changed marketing in a variety of ways. These include:

Customer service is 24/7 – Customer service was starting to lose its meaning before the digital age. Today, customers expect you to address their needs no matter what the day or time.

A more level playing field – Digital marketing channels are now more level than before as digital marketing channels provide as much coverage to smaller companies as they do to name brands.

Pay to play is coming back – In the past, the company with the biggest advertising budget usually won. At the start of the digital age, free advertising was everywhere, but today, social media channels have brought back pay to play with most companies, large and small, having a budget for reaching people via social media.

It's hurting traditional advertising – As people are moving online, television and radio audiences have fallen thanks in some part to the many streaming services that are now available.

Ads can't just be ads anymore – Conventional advertisement is no longer viable as online, pop-up ad blockers are common, and even when ads do appear, they tend to be ignored through a phenomenon known as "ad blindness". As a result, digital marketing channels often give something before they can get something back such as a free eBook or entry into a competition.

This has both revolutionized small businesses, while at the same time challenging large businesses [Agrawal, 2016].

Now let's look at some case studies to see some best practices in this new and constantly evolving environment.

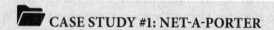 **CASE STUDY #1: NET-A-PORTER**

CHALLENGE

Net-a-Porter is an online-only luxury clothing store. For their brand to become a leading online luxury brand they needed to improve sales, increase brand loyalty, and create lasting customer relationships.

However, they had to overcome two challenges first. They were:

1. Most of their competition online wanted to position themselves either as luxury or the best online brand.
2. Online customers tend to try to find the best deal, often switching brands to do so.

APPROACH

To overcome these challenges, they had to position themselves as a luxury business, based on quality, not price.

Their approach included using three distinct channels:

1. Mobile app/social network – To keep customers inside their ecosystem.
2. Email marketing – To make sure that they followed up on customer behavior on their site.
3. Ad re-targeting – To catch visitors who left their site before buying.

Their approach included their "Net Set" app which allows users to interact with each other and share images with each other. It also recognizes which products are being shared, finds the closest match in Net-a-Porter's inventory, and recommends it to users so they can buy it.

They felt it was important that customers experience all of their channels, so they sent out email reminders or messages in the app to connect on their other channels.

RESULTS

At least partially as a result of using this approach, Net-a-Porter had revenues of more than $3 billion in 2017 alone, with 16.9 percent year-over-year growth.

Furthermore, 50 percent of their sales came from mobile, with the rest from email marketing, retargeting, organic, and other channels.

Finally, their average order value increased to about $400, which is one of the highest for any online store, even more than Amazon [Meyer, 2018].

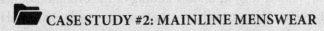 **CASE STUDY #2: MAINLINE MENSWEAR**

CHALLENGE

Mainline Menswear, founded in 2004, is a British e-commerce business focused on men's fashion that wanted to increase their sales primarily by increasing traffic to their website.

APPROACH

Mainline Menswear face increasing competition from similar brands on the Web, and as a result decided to use an omni-channel marketing approach to become more creative and resourceful than their competition.

Using mobile technology for their winter sale in 2013 (Boxing Day), Mainline Menswear decided to use a combination of coupons/promotions via SMS, re-target ads, and cart abandonment emails.

Instead of using just one channel (email), they decided to use multiple channels in a seamless campaign, where users would have a connected experience on all three channels.

RESULTS

On Boxing Day 2013, Mainline Menswear sent a sales campaign via SMS, instead of the usual email campaigns they had used in the past. Mainline Menswear saw the following results:

- Forty-five percent increase in direct traffic.
- Twenty-seven percent rise in overall traffic.
- Ninety-three percent boost in their mobile traffic.

Ultimately, the campaign led to one of the busiest days in Mainline Menswear's entire history.

In the end, by utilizing the omni-channel approach, Mainline lowered their average customer acquisition cost ... an approach they've utilized many times since [Meyer, 2018].

Now that we have a good understanding of the evolution of marketing through the years, it's time to discuss the basics of supply chain and logistics management followed by the impact of the Internet and e-commerce on it.

Part III

Traditional vs. Omni-Channel Distribution

6

Supply Chain and Logistics 101

Over the past 25 years alone, the supply chain and logistics field has gone from one that was a mystery to most people, to the point today where we see (UPS) commercials with people singing "I Love Logistics".

As the saying goes, "if one wants to define the future, they must study the past" [Confucius, 551 BC–479 BC]. So before getting into strategy, let's first discuss supply chain and logistics from an historical perspective and then analyze the impact that the Internet and e-commerce have had on the field.

HISTORICAL PERSPECTIVE

Until after World War II, logistics was thought of in military terms for the most part as the link that supplied troops with rations, weapons, and equipment.

Up to that point, within business organizations, logistics was fragmented, primarily focusing on transportation and purchasing.

In educational institutions, there were no integrated programs. Instead individual courses were offered in transportation and purchasing.

After World War II, as businesses began to understand the relationships and tradeoffs such as inventory costs vs. transportation costs, which will be discussed later, logistics gained an important place in the business world as well.

In the 1960s physical distribution, a more integrated concept that included activities such as transportation, inventory control, warehousing, and facility location, became an area of study and practice in education and industry. Physical distribution involved the coordination of more than one activity associated with supplying product to the marketplace (i.e. more focused on the "outbound" side of manufacturing).

By the mid-1960s, the scope of physical distribution was expanded to include the supply side including inbound transportation and warehousing and was referred to as business logistics. In many cases, purchasing was not included and went under the heading of "materials management" or "procurement".

In the early 1980s as American manufacturing had been hammered by overseas competitors for over a decade and began actively outsourcing materials, labor, and manufacturing overseas, the term "supply chain management" entered the common business lexicon. It defined both the new, complex global world we now live and do business in, as well as an understanding of the integration and importance of all activities involved in sourcing and procurement, conversion, and logistics management. This includes the coordination and collaboration with channel partners, which can be suppliers, intermediaries, third-party service providers, and customers.

As opposed to the past, where physical distribution, logistics, purchasing, etc., were all fragmented, many of today's organizations feature an integrated supply chain organization, in most cases led by a senior-level executive (Figure 6.1).

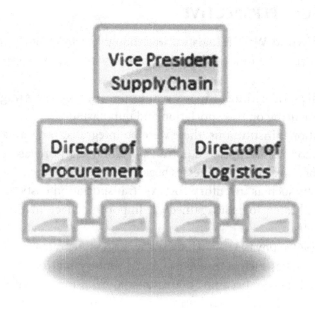

FIGURE 6.1
Supply chain organizational chart.

Technology has helped to drive the concept of an integrated supply chain starting with the development of electronic data interchange (EDI) systems as a standardized format for the electronic transfer of data between business enterprises (which really took off in the 1980s), as well as the introduction of "off the shelf" enterprise resource planning (ERP) software systems which featured integrated core business processes in a common database. Furthering this into the 21st century has been the expansion of Internet-based collaborative systems not only internally within an organization but often with customers, suppliers, and other partners.

This supply chain evolution has resulted in both increasing value added and cost reductions through integration and collaboration.

ORGANIZATIONAL AND SUPPLY CHAIN STRATEGY

As was discussed in Chapter 2, both retailers and wholesalers are "intermediaries" and provide a utility or value to the customer.

Utility refers to the value or benefit a customer receives from a purchase. There are four basic types of utility: Form, place, time, and possession, and more recently, the utilities of information and service have been added.

Supply chain management contributes to all of these utilities, as it's all about having the "right product, at the right place and price, at the right time".

If an organization can identify what adds value for their customers and deliver it successfully, they will have established a competitive advantage, which, in essence, is the purpose of a strategic plan.

Mission Statement

In order to create a strategic plan you must first establish a broad mission statement, supported by specific objectives for your business. A mission statement is a company's purpose or "reason for being" and should guide the actions of the organization, lay out its overall goal, providing a path, and guiding decision-making.

It doesn't have to be lengthy, but should be well thought out and touch on the following concepts:

- Customers: Who are our customers?
- Products or services: Major products or services.

- Markets: Where do we compete?
- Technology: What is our basic technology?
- Future survival, growth, and profitability: Our commitment towards economic objectives.
- Philosophy: The basic beliefs, core values, aspirations, and philosophical priorities of the firm.
- Self-concept: Identify the firm's major strengths and competitive advantages.
- Public image: What is our public image?
- Concern for employees: Our attitude towards employees.

Objectives

The mission is a broad statement but should then lead to specific objectives with measurable targets that a firm can use to evaluate the extent to which it achieves its mission.

In a typical medium- to large-size organization, individual functions/ departments may have their own mission statements, but most at least have goals and objectives that are tied to the company's overall mission statement and objectives (see example in Figure 6.2).

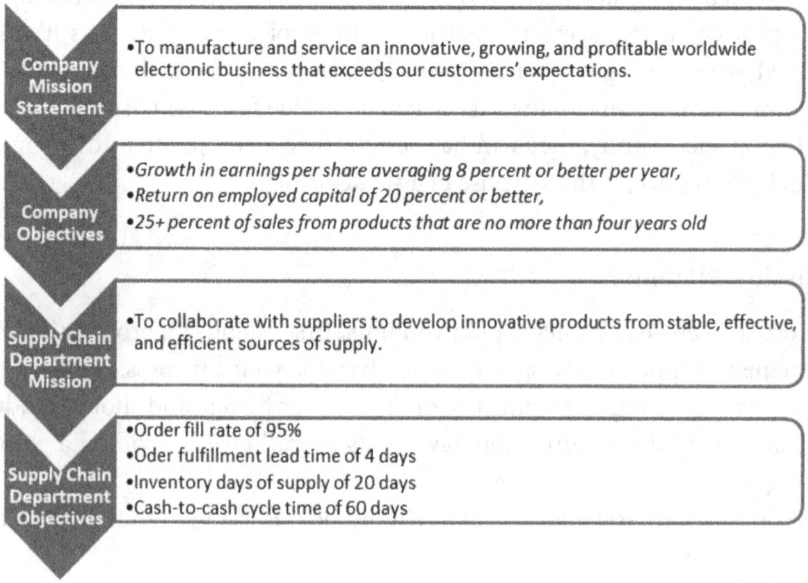

Company Mission Statement
- To manufacture and service an innovative, growing, and profitable worldwide electronic business that exceeds our customers' expectations.

Company Objectives
- *Growth in earnings per share averaging 8 percent or better per year,*
- *Return on employed capital of 20 percent or better,*
- *25+ percent of sales from products that are no more than four years old*

Supply Chain Department Mission
- To collaborate with suppliers to develop innovative products from stable, effective, and efficient sources of supply.

Supply Chain Department Objectives
- Order fill rate of 95%
- Oder fulfillment lead time of 4 days
- Inventory days of supply of 20 days
- Cash-to-cash cycle time of 60 days

FIGURE 6.2
Sample company and supply chain mission statements and objectives.

SWOT Analysis

After specifying the objectives for a business, an organization should perform a strengths, weaknesses, opportunities, and threats (SWOT) analysis to determine strategic choices for the organization to establish a competitive advantage (also used in developing functional strategies such as supply chain as well as marketing, which was discussed in Chapter 4).

To refresh, the components of a SWOT analysis are described as:

- Strengths – Resources and capabilities that can be used as a basis for developing a competitive advantage.
- Weaknesses – Characteristics that place the business or project at a disadvantage relative to other businesses.
- Opportunities – External environmental analysis may reveal certain new opportunities for profit and growth.
- Threats – Changes in the external environmental also may present threats to the firm.

Using the SWOT framework, you can start to develop a strategy that helps you distinguish your organization from your competitors, so that you can compete successfully in your market(s).

Strategic Choices

Strategic choices will be made based upon the results of the SWOT analysis and can fall into the competitive priority categories of cost, quality, time, or flexibility [Krajewski et al., 2013].

Cost strategy – Focuses on delivering a product or service to the customer at the lowest possible cost without sacrificing quality. To reduce costs, processes must be efficiently designed and operated often using tools such as process analysis. Walmart has been the low-cost leader in retail by operating an efficient supply chain.

Time strategy – This strategy can be in terms of speed of delivery, response time, or even product development time. Processes should be designed and planned to minimize and standardize lead times. Dell has been a prime example of a manufacturer that has excelled at response time by assembling, testing, and shipping computers in as little as a few days. FedEx is known for fast, on-time deliveries of small packages.

Quality strategy – To deliver on the promise of consistent, high-quality goods or services requires a reliable, safe supply chain. Processes should be designed and run to minimize errors and defects. If Sony had an inferior supply chain with high damage levels, it wouldn't matter to the customer that their electronics are of the highest quality.

Flexibility strategy – Can come in various forms such as volume, variety, and customization. Many of today's e-commerce businesses such as Amazon offer a great deal of flexibility in many of these categories.

In many cases, an organization may focus on more than one of the above strategies, and even when focusing on one, it doesn't mean that they will offer sub-par performance on the others (just not "best in class" perhaps).

The supply chain must then be aligned and managed to support these strategies.

SUPPLY CHAIN OPPORTUNITIES AND CHALLENGES

When considering a supply chain strategy, it is important to be aware of current opportunities and challenges.

We live in volatile times. There are many external threats to our supply chain now and in the future. A white paper by Hitachi Consulting [Hitachi, 2009] identified "Six Key Trends Changing Supply Chain Management Today":

1. Demand planning – Companies are moving more towards a "make what you sell" demand or pull-driven process and are trying to influence and manage demand better. Cross-functional processes such as sales and operations planning (S&OP) which will be discussed later in this text help to improve awareness, coordination,

and accuracy of demand estimates to ultimately improve customer service while reducing costs.

Organizations that don't wrap their minds around this will continue to struggle with meeting increasingly volatile demand, which in many cases is caused by incentives, promotions, and external factors such as COVID-19, resulting in manufacturing (and purchasing) reacting after the fact and producing larger than needed lot sizes which are "pushed" through the supply chain causing inefficiencies throughout. This is known as the "bullwhip" effect (see Figure 6.3) which describes the magnification (especially on inventory, operational costs, and customer service) that occurs when variations in customer demand move up the supply chain. It can be caused by a variety of things such as forecast errors, large lot sizes, long setups, panic ordering, variance in lead times, etc.

We will discuss ways to combat the bullwhip effect in Chapter 15 by using lean techniques and tools such to reduce production and distribution "pushing" of large batches, electronic data interchange (EDI) to avoid batching of orders, collaboration programs such as vendor-managed inventory (VMI) and collaborative planning, forecasting, and replenishment (CPFR) collaborate with customers and suppliers to share information, everyday low pricing (EDLP), and so on.

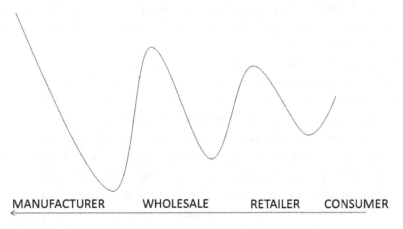

MANUFACTURER   WHOLESALE   RETAILER   CONSUMER

FIGURE 6.3
The bullwhip effect.

2. Globalization – No area of business is more impacted by globalization than the supply chain. The benefits to globalization include access to more markets, a larger supplier pool, a greater selection of employees, etc. On the downside are the various risks that we mentioned earlier.

   Supply chain network design is important in managing the changes brought about by globalization and can optimize the number, location, size, and type of facilities and flow of materials throughout the network.

3. Increased competition and price pressures – The commoditization of many products has forced businesses to find better ways to distinguish themselves. They now look to the supply chain to reduce cost and add value for the customer through both the product and service.

   Cost improvements can be found through:
   - Sales and operations planning
   - Transportation/distribution management
   - Improved product lifecycle management
   - Improved strategic sourcing and procurement

   Value-added service can be provided through:
   - Vendor-managed inventory (VMI) – Buyer of a product provides information to a vendor and the supplier takes full responsibility for maintaining an agreed inventory of the material, usually at the buyer's consumption location.
   - Radio-frequency identification (RFID) – The wireless use of radio-frequency to transfer data, to identify and track tags attached to objects.
   - Labeling and packaging.
   - Drop shipping.
   - Collaboration.

4. Outsourcing – The supply chain and logistics functions are always a good candidate for outsourcing as they may not be a core competency for an organization. There is of course the tradeoff of risk and reward which requires good supply chain network design integration with the outsourcing partner in the information chain, and control mechanisms to monitor the various components of the supply chain with information systems that connect and coordinate the entire supply chain.

5. Shortened and more complex product lifecycles – Today there is increasing pressure to develop and introduce new and innovative products quickly. To do this companies have worked on improving their product lifecycle management (PLM) processes. The benefits of PLM to the supply chain include processes and technology to design products that can share common operations, components, or materials with other products. This can reduce the risk of obsolescence and reduce costs when purchasing key materials. A formalized PLM process can also help to coordinate marketing, engineering, sales, and procurement and develop sales forecasts to plan products that are in a company's pipeline.
6. Closer integration and collaboration with supplier – Supply chain collaboration is more than just connecting information systems and now extends to fully integrating business processes and organization structures across companies that make up the entire value chain.

   S&OP processes now extend to an organization's external supply chain partners to include demand information, such as customer forecasts, and supply information, such as supplier inventories and capacities.

As the supply chain has become more global and complex in nature, technology has advanced to help manage the process and comes under the heading of systems such as enterprise resource planning (ERP), supply chain management (SCM), and supply chain planning (SCP) systems.

These systems enable processes such as:

- Network and inventory optimization
- Logistics optimization
- Product lifecycle management
- Sales and operations planning
- Procurement
- Manufacturing optimization
- Warehouse operations
- Business intelligence

I would also add the trend of companies that have started applying lean and Six Sigma concepts to the extended supply chain. These are both team-based continuous improvement processes; lean helps to identify and eliminate waste throughout an organization, and Six Sigma reduces variation in individual processes. As they are somewhat complementary, they have now, in many cases, been combined as "Lean Six Sigma".

There is also the challenge of sustainability as resources have become increasingly constrained due to the global economy as well as climate change, helping to create regulations that governments have put into place in an effort to minimize damage to the environment.

Of course, the "elephant in the room" (and seventh major trend), as far as opportunities and challenges go, is omni-channel marketing and retailing.

SEGMENTING THE SUPPLY CHAIN

Today's use of omni-channel marketing and retailing, which, as previously mentioned, is an integrated approach of selling to consumers through multiple distribution channels (i.e. brick-and-mortar, mobile Internet devices, computers, television, radio, direct mail, catalog, etc.), has created the need to handle multiple channels with separate warehouse picking operations, often replenished from a common inventory in a single facility.

This can lead many companies, such as Dell, to segment their entire supply chains whereby different channels and products are served through different supply chain processes. The ultimate goal is to determine the best supply chain processes and policies for individual customers and products that also maximize customer service and company profitability.

The rationale for this, according to an Ernst & Young white paper entitled "Supply Chain Segmentation", is that the "business environment is getting increasingly complex, especially for technology companies dealing with rapid innovation, globalization and a growing number of business partners, business models and differences in expectations from different markets and customers" [www.ey.com, 2014].

E&Y suggest five ways to consider segmentation:

1. Product complexity-based
2. Supply chain risk-based
3. Manufacturing process and technology-based

4. Customer service needs-based
5. Market-driven

The idea is that a "one-size-fits-all" strategy will not usually work in today's environment.

They suggest that while senior sponsorship is required for successful supply chain segmentation, you also need cross-functional support from multiple organizational disciplines. The team must provide supporting policies, segment-level processes, and IT infrastructure to both automate the processes and provide metrics.

In Dell's case, over the past few years, they have expanded beyond their direct-to-customer model to a "multichannel, segmented model, with different policies for serving consumers, corporate customers, distributors, and retailers. Through this transformation, Dell has saved US $1.5 billion in operational costs" [Thomas, 2012].

The past 25 years or so have been the most challenging and exciting of times in the supply chain world with the growth of the global economy, which to some extent has been enabled and managed by the creation of the Internet and subsequent growth of e-commerce and other hardware and software developments. All of this will be discussed in the next chapter.

7

The Internet and the Emergence of E-Commerce and Their Impact on Traditional Supply Chain and Logistics

In the early 1980s, as companies found the need to source and manufacture globally to compete in an emerging global economy, the term "supply chain", not totally coincidentally, was coined as a way to describe the need to integrate their major business processes, internally and externally, from the customer to an extended network of global suppliers.

Luckily, this coincided with the invention of the personal computer which gave better access to professionals in the field, with new tools such as spreadsheets and graphical-based interfaces helping to significantly improve supply chain and logistics planning and execution technology.

At this time, executives began to realize that if they were willing to invest in training and new technology in this field, they could significantly improve profitability and customer service.

This led to the development in the late 1980s and early 1990s of what came to be known as enterprise resource planning (ERP) systems, which enabled the integrated management of core business (largely transactional) processes.

ERP systems are a suite of integrated business applications, which have grown to include most major functions such as accounting, manufacturing, supply chain and logistics, operations, human resources, customer relationships management, etc. Organization use them to collect, store, manage, and interpret data from these various business activities.

ERP software also increased the recognition of the need for better planning and integration, which resulted in the creation of advanced planning and scheduling (APS) software in the functional areas of manufacturing, operations, and supply chain and logistics.

By the 1990s, the Internet began to emerge for commercial use, many years after the creation of he Advanced Research Projects Agency Network (ARPANET), funded by the U.S. Department of Defense in the late 1960s. ARPANET used "packet switching" where a message is broken into a number of parts which are sent independently over whatever route is optimum for each packet and reassembled at the destination, allowing multiple computers to communicate on a single network.

IMPACT OF THE INTERNET ON THE SUPPLY CHAIN

Many ERP and APS systems went from being installed on company's servers to becoming "Web-enabled" to then many becoming "Web-based", all of which has had a significant impact on cost reduction, collaboration, and customer service.

The initial impact of the Internet on the supply chain involved communications such as email and tracking and tracing shipments.

Today, the impact of the Web on the supply chain has grown exponentially and can be seen in six major areas:

  Inventory management – The Internet has made it much easier for businesses to quickly set up Web-based electronic data interchange (EDI) information programs with their clients. Before the emergence of the Internet, EDI could take quite a bit of time to be implemented in a supply chain as each channel member had to invest significant funds in software, equipment, and training before EDI systems could be made operational.

  Purchasing – The Internet has made it possible for costs associated with purchasing to be reduced as many companies have used the Internet to streamline their purchasing functions, resulting in reductions in paper-flows and order cycle times. This has also resulted in a reduction in the need for face-to-face negotiations, as much of it can now be done via the Internet.

  Transportation – This is one of the most popular uses of the Internet in supply chains as the tracking and tracing of shipments provide the firm with data that show it the reliability of the performance of its carriers. It also enables the firm to inform facilities and customers about shipment delays as they occur rather than waiting for days or even longer before informing them.

Order processing – The Internet has helped to dramatically reduce order processing costs and cycle times. The reduction in paperwork is a major item of this cost saving when compared to conventional practices, and there is now a reduction in the time it takes for orders to be placed and processed and for products to be received by clients (and for the entire order-to-pay cycle). This has brought order cycle times from up to a week or more in the past, down to next-day or even same-day processing and shipping (and in some cases delivery) today.

Vendor relationships – The Internet has been used to better monitor the performance of its vendors in areas such as deliveries to the company's warehouses, raw material conformance to quality, and other agreed-upon measures.

Customer service – The Internet has made it possible for customers to have 24-hour access to a company's customer service department, making it possible for companies to be notified of any problem or service issue in real time. Besides providing another option for customers to contact a company concerning service issues, this has helped improve communication flow between businesses and their customers [Miller, 2013].

Furthermore, the Internet has greatly impacted forecasting and deployment planning as everything from customer and remote sales personnel input, point of sale (POS) data, social media, and even the weather can impact supply chain planning and operations.

IMPACT OF E-COMMERCE ON THE SUPPLY CHAIN

Simply put, e-commerce (or electronic commerce) is the buying and selling of goods (or services) on the Internet.

E-commerce encompasses a wide variety of data, systems, and tools for both online buyers and sellers ranging from desktop and mobile shopping to online payment encryption and beyond.

Businesses with an e-commerce model typically use an e-commerce store and/or an e-commerce platform to perform online marketing and sales activities and to manage logistics and fulfillment.

Major E-Commerce Models

The main models of e-commerce that businesses are most concerned with are business-to-consumer (B2C) and business-to-business (B2B).

> Business-to-consumer (B2C) – This encompasses transactions made between a business and a consumer. This is one of the most widely used sales models in the e-commerce context. When you buy electronics from an online electronics retailer, it is a business-to-consumer transaction.
>
> Business-to-business (B2B) – This relates to sales made between businesses, such as a manufacturer and a wholesaler or retailer. This type of e-commerce is not consumer-facing and happens only between business entities. Most often, business-to-business sales focus on raw materials or products that are repackaged or combined and sold to other businesses before being sold to customers.

It should be noted that in 2017, the global market size of B2B was estimated to be $7.7 trillion, and that of B2C was $2.1 trillion.

There are in total nine e-commerce models (see Table 7.1) such as business-to-government (B2G) for businesses whose sole clients are governments

TABLE 7.1

E-Commerce Models

	Government	Business	Consumer
Government	G2G e.g. central and state	G2B e-Tenders	G2C Information to citizens, online forms
Business	B2G e.g. procurement	B2B Covisint.com, EDI, EFT	B2C Amazon.com Walmart.com
Consumer	C2G Online filing of tax returns	C2B Job portals like indeed.com	C2C Facebook.com eBay.com

Source: OECD.org, i.e. Organization for Economic Co-operation and Development.

or type of public administration, and consumer-to-consumer (C2C) such as eBay, Craigslist, and numerous other auction and classified sites where customers trade, buy, and sell items in exchange for a small commission paid to the site.

E-Commerce Has Complicated Things for Retailers and Manufacturers

Retail supply chains and global retail sourcing are to this day still being impacted by the ongoing rapid growth of e-commerce. The Internet has created better global supply chain visibility for both buyers and sellers, bringing them much closer together and making them more easily connected. It is fairly common today for someone to buy products directly from a manufacturer in China with no minimum order quantity and have them delivered in a less than a month to anywhere in the world. This has both created new opportunities and disrupted traditional business models.

Impact on Retail

Furthermore, larger retailers such as Walmart and Best Buy have e-marketplaces where third-party vendors can list and sell their products. There are also niche marketplaces that disrupt a variety of retail categories such as eyeglasses and cosmetics, allowing vendors to sell direct to their customers without traditional marketing and distribution channels where manufacturers would sell to wholesalers, retailers and brands, or other intermediaries, who then sell to the consumer or end user.

Additionally, as traditional retailers and brands expand through online and social channels, online retailers are growing their physical presence in the trend known as "click and mortar".

For example, Walmart purchased a 77 percent stake in Indian e-commerce company Flipkart for $16 billion to help their global sourcing from India, while at the same time giving Walmart access to India's massive retail market, and to help them take on Amazon in the growing Indian market.

This has created greater complexity in the retail supply chain as companies need to create infrastructure to support all their channels while, at the same time, maintaining lean, agile supply chains.

Impact on Manufacturers

Many manufacturers are building direct-to-consumer channels, bypassing the middleman, creating additional revenue with a leaner and faster retail supply chain such as Nike, which, in some cases, skips their traditional retailers and sells through their own stores and website.

Manufacturers are also utilizing a direct-store-delivery (DSD) model, by-passing the retailer's distribution channels, enabling them to be more responsive to the customer.

E-commerce is also impacting B2B (an $8 trillion market in the United States alone). One such example is the growth of Amazon Business, with over a million business customers and 100,000 sellers of business supplies, which is attempting to reduce inefficiencies in purchasing organizations by making it easier for employees to buy products with a similar buying experience as that found in B2C.

Many B2B suppliers, ranging from wholesale producers to governments, health care, etc., are making their products available on the Amazon channel, having Amazon act as a broker for B2B sales channels. Forrester Research estimates that up to one million U.S. B2B salespeople will lose their jobs to self-service e-commerce by the year 2020.

E-commerce growth brings different challenges to the global sourcing function as consumers are now used to improved service, quality, delivery times, availability, and price. Trends are changing more quickly, requiring shorter product cycle times and more effective supplier management with the possibility of increased returns and greater competition.

Managing the transition from a physical to an online channel is a huge challenge for sourcing executives as they need to manage and optimize inventory and transportation work in both the "brick-and-mortar" and the online environment.

Ultimately, retailers and manufacturers need a more sophisticated supply chain management process with greater supplier collaboration and more sophisticated technology to enable visibility, efficiency, and speed in increasingly complex supply chains. This is especially critical in the coming years as:

- Digital commerce accounts for only 10 percent of the $5 trillion in total annual retail sales but is predicted to grow to 17.5 percent by 2021 (of total retail).

- B2C e-commerce sales are expected to grow from $2.3 trillion, to $4.5 trillion by 2021.
- The B2B market will exceed $7.7 trillion in 2018 (three times the size of B2C) with B2B e-commerce alone expected to reach $1 trillion by 2020, 12 percent of all U.S. B2B sales [Beron, 2018].

E-COMMERCE IS EVEN DRIVING THE INDUSTRIAL REAL ESTATE MARKET

One doesn't often think about the intersection of supply chain management and real estate, but the relationship goes back a long way in the distribution and warehouse function, and now with the shift towards e-commerce, it is more important and visible than ever before.

In fact, regional distribution facilities are the most common property type in the U.S., comprising well over 60 percent of the U.S. industrial inventory and the majority of industrial REIT portfolios, according to an article in Wealth Management Magazine.

E-commerce retailers use logistics real estate in ways that require more space. Many activities that were typically carried out within stores are now consolidated into logistics facilities, and e-commerce customers just need more room, as much as three times as much or more logistics space as their brick-and-mortar counterparts.

The "location decision" is now more than ever a strategy that shouldn't be taken lightly and should be looked at in terms of:

Sourcing – An organization must decide if they plan to fulfill e-commerce orders from the store, a distribution center (DC) dedicated to fulfilling e-commerce orders with a separate DC dedicated to their stores, or one DC that fulfills both the e-commerce orders and replenishes store inventory. In many cases, companies may choose to have a combination of these methods.

Location – In many cases with e-commerce, it is important to reach most consumers in the least amount of time due to the requirements of overnight or even same-day shipments. So there has been an increase in the number of retailers headed toward urban hubs like New Jersey, Lehigh Valley, and southern California which are near major metropolitan areas. It is also critical to consider labor availability in the area, especially during the holiday season.

Develop or adapt – The type of facility you choose can depend on your business objectives and specific current and future needs (often customized), which may push the decision towards either a new building or finding an existing building.

Design – E-commerce has specific and different requirements than traditional DCs such as they may be more automated but still require a vast amount of labor for "pick and pack" vs. "pallet in, pallet/case out" traditional DCs with a high variety of items.

Each company needs to determine its own needs for capital investment, length of commitment, and anticipated rate of change in its business to determine its particular e-commerce real estate strategy, but there is no denying that e-commerce is driving the need for industrial real estate and is now a critical part of the competitive and location strategy of many companies today [Myerson, 2016].

While multi-channel retail is approaching maturity many years after the emergence of e-commerce, most companies are still figuring out how to provide a seamless omni-channel retail experience supported by their supply chain, as described in our next chapter.

8

Omni-Channel Supply Chain Challenges

Omni-channel retail means consumers want the same experience across all retail channels. However, while most customers want to view in-store inventory online and to be able to buy online and pickup in-store, only around a third of retailers can perform those basic omni-channel functions. On top of that, retailers must enable customers to choose how to return goods (i.e. ship back or return to stores).

Omni-channel retailing involves seamlessly integrating the customer experience across all interaction channels – in-store, on the Web, and on mobile devices.

The buying process is less predictable and more dynamic, through increasing Internet and mobile use, with more "touchpoints". Consumers have also become more powerful partially due to social media.

While we can more easily see this in the B2C (retail) sector, the B2B (manufacturer and wholesaler/distributor) sector also has to deal with more complex transactions and processes with a variety of partners, customers, and suppliers having to be integrated.

WHY IS OMNI-CHANNEL IMPORTANT?

The changing needs and desires of today's consumer (especially millennials) have put added stress on the retail supply chain.

Omni-channel, when executed properly, can help to meet these demands as consumers love omni-channel retail since it is easy to customize delivery choice, they have more chances to check an item before purchase, they feel safe to purchase items, and it's a way to access the store's products conveniently.

Furthermore, consumers want quick and correct delivery. While two days was considered fast a few years ago, many today can hardly wait two hours.

An added advantage of omni-channel is that it has the potential to increase sales as it can add new customers and new sales channels.

So, while there are great challenges and opportunities with omni-channel retail, they have a great variety of impacts on the supply chain that need to be dealt with.

THE IMPACT OF OMNI-CHANNEL COMMERCE ON THE RETAIL SUPPLY CHAIN

Today's customers expect a consistent buying experience across all retail channels. This has significant impacts on the retail supply chain in a variety of areas.

Processing Customer Orders

A tradition retail supply chain is hierarchical, with complete customer demand fulfilled at the store. Shifting that volume of sales to a B2C channel requires filling a truck with boxes holding only one to five items, and many thousands of boxes a day. The major impact is to increase the number of deliveries exponentially while decreasing the number of line items in the system.

Furthermore, the volatility of online ordering requires companies to broaden the portfolio of items they keep in stock to maximize customer demand, so retailers must broaden the portfolio of stock-keeping units and reduce the number of delivery lines shipped per delivery.

For example, in the recent past, a shoe retailer running a shop needed to have approximately 100 types of shoes to meet demand. Today, with Zappos and shoes.com offering over 20,000 types, to stay competitive, the same shoe retailer needs to be able to offer and ship almost every brand and type of shoe (and they need to also carry the most popular shoe sizes).

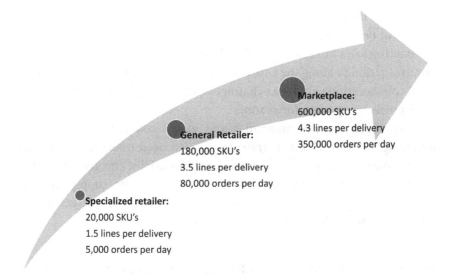

Marketplace:
600,000 SKU's
4.3 lines per delivery
350,000 orders per day

General Retailer:
180,000 SKU's
3.5 lines per delivery
80,000 orders per day

Specialized retailer:
20,000 SKU's
1.5 lines per delivery
5,000 orders per day

FIGURE 8.1
Fundamental effects of e-commerce engagement on a traditional retailer's supply chain.
(Source: Kourimsky and van der Berk, 2014.)

So, when adding an e-commerce component, the brick-and-mortar shoe store has exponentially more orders and SKUs to manage (see Figure 8.1).

Delivery from Store or Distribution Center?

Implementing an omni-channel process usually requires creating or enhancing a "standard" e-commerce strategy, as at some point the company needs to halt the distribution process and ship goods directly to the customer (usually at the DC).

As stores may be supplied from several distribution centers, a customer order might need to be fulfilled from several distribution centers.

Delivery from a store to the customer may be easier than from a DC, depending on transportation cost, picking efficiency, trained manpower, etc. So, supply chain organizations must choose between the two models (or use some combination of both).

Inventory Optimization and Sales and Operations Planning

One of the critical challenges of implementing an omni-channel process is that the safety stock levels and stock deployment must be re-determined throughout the supply chain. Sales forecasts will have to adapt, and service levels will need to be re-evaluated.

Adapting sales forecasts to include both store and e-commerce demand requires visibility along the entire supply chain. Additional data can come from collaboration with other channels such as distributors or from social media measuring tools, for example.

Given today's market dynamics and global competition, companies following an omni-channel strategy will also need to explore new ways to optimize inventory which can be supported by effective sales and operations planning (i.e. making sure that aggregate supply matches demand) assisted by demand-sensing tools that combine next-generation forecasting methods with "big data" technologies.

Impacts on Distribution/Fulfillment Centers and IT

Most companies will want to adapt their distribution center to deliver B2C orders, at the very least due to transportation, workforce, and process issues with new areas set up for packing stations (vs. traditionally shipping cases and sometimes full pallets of individual SKUs out) and consolidation.

Distribution centers may even need to be relocated to cover a wider variety of goods, in some cases (thus the reason for a "hot" e-commerce industrial real estate market discussed in Chapter 7).

The foundation of providing an omni-channel experience starts with a company's core technology. The ability to deliver an omni-channel experience rests on having a single commerce platform that unifies front-end and back-end systems, and provides a central hub for order management, customer, item, and inventory data. The back-end systems of the platform will then funnel data to all sales channels, ensuring that accurate information across all customer touchpoints is delivered in real time, creating efficiencies and opportunities to improve the customer experience.

Real-time visibility of inventory levels across all channels means you will never miss out on sales opportunities because of inadequately stocked merchandise and inefficient modes of tracking product levels. Centralized order management delivers on the promise of fulfilling, buying, and returning anywhere. And unifying siloed sources of customer data into a single repository to get one complete view of the customer across all channels and touchpoints will deliver consistent customer service and support personalized marketing, merchandising, and targeted promotions across all channels.

Specifically, there will be a large impact on warehouse IT processes, as modifying traditional warehouse processes to handle the increased-volume, smaller sized "pick and pack" Web-based orders is just one of the many impacts that the warehouse management system will face.

Making the received goods available for immediate sale is a key challenge for e-commerce retailers.

At Amazon, for example, incoming goods are immediately put into the closest available bin. They unload and put away the goods as fast as possible (versus up to 3 days at some DCs), even putting cosmetics, shoes, and books in the same storage bin. This helps to reduce stock levels in the distribution centers and free up cash.

Impact of a Multi-Step Picking Process

Distribution centers will not only have to look at physical layout and receiving process, but they will have to adapt their shipping operations significantly.

Internet orders are much smaller and more numerous than B2B processes, so the distribution center will typically have to set up a multi-step picking process (Figure 8.2). Picking will usually be "consolidated", where a warehouse operator will pick for several sales orders at a time. These items will be conveyed to a packing station where the consolidated picks will be sorted and packed into a box for the end customer, and finally loaded onto the correct carrier vehicle [Kourimsky and van der Berk, 2014].

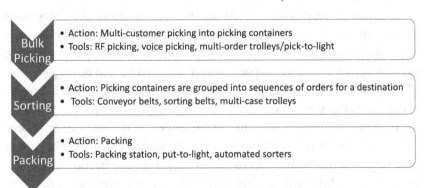

FIGURE 8.2
Best practice for B2C picking. (Source: Kourimsky and van der Berk, 2014.)

THE IMPACT OF OMNI-CHANNEL COMMERCE ON MANUFACTURERS

While a lot of the focus on omni-channel has been on retail, it's easy to lose sight of the impact on manufacturing.

Even before omni-channel became a "hot" topic, manufacturers were focusing on having timely and accurate visibility of retail demand and consumption on the production line, distribution center, and store in order to fulfill orders on time and at the lowest cost possible. So omni-channel is just an extension of that effort, and as a result, at least to some extent, the B2B and B2C sides of e-commerce are merging.

An omni-channel solution is practically impossible without e-commerce, and vice-versa in the case of manufacturers. Customers want to be able to have options and maintain accountability with the manufacturer at practically any stage in the shipping and order process.

The traditional way of manufacturers selling to retail only is rapidly being supplanted by the idea of working in an integrated and collaborative omni-channel environment, including e-commerce, in order to survive and thrive.

Key Challenges

The consumer today is everywhere and has a large impact on the entire supply chain, all the way down to the manufacturing level. As a result, consumers now expect an endless assortment of goods that reaches all the way up to the manufacturer.

Organizations must bring on additional items or variations of existing items (such as more sizes or colors) and make those items available anywhere, at any time according to the customer's increasing demand for personalization and customization. So, the impact on the manufacturer can be huge.

Furthermore, the distinction between brands and retailers doesn't concern most consumers. Smart manufacturers can take advantage of this opportunity to get closer to the consumer. However, they will need the required fulfillment and supply chain capabilities, which is the case as some larger brands such as LG and L'Oréal are creating frictionless direct-to-consumer fulfillment options. Currently, manufacturer sales direct to consumers are under 10 percent of revenue, but with less resistance from retailers, there is opportunity to grow this channel.

Manufacturers must react to more frequent, smaller orders of more items. Some manufacturers are now even being asked to drop-ship programs, which requires the manufacturer to act as a direct-to-consumer company.

This results in a reduction in the number of single SKU pallets, complicating the pick and pack process, with increased flexibility and planning required as well as more labor for preparing goods for shipment.

Manufacturers must become more flexible and agile in fulfilling orders to ensure on-time and accurate customer deliveries. They also must gain visibility beyond the factory into distribution centers and across the entire supply chain to track raw materials, works in progress, and finished goods while also managing new pick/pack operations and shipping processes. Transportation routing must be efficiently planned, trailers must be efficiently loaded with contents that don't necessarily align and stack like pallets, and the increasing number of trailer appointments due to smaller orders with mixed items must be managed to minimize congestion at the yard.

Ultimately, to stay competitive in the emerging omni-channel world, manufacturers must adapt their processes as well as their systems to the new lean, agile world of omni-channel retail.

OMNI-CHANNEL SUPPLY CHAIN CASES

CASE STUDY #1: HOW HOME DEPOT NAILS OMNI-CHANNEL SUPPLY CHAIN FULFILLMENT

CHALLENGE

Home Depot is the largest home improvement retailer in the United States. They have had a lot of success with their e-commerce business, as in 2016 they had sales of $4.6 billion (a 25 percent increase from the previous year and 2.5 times what they did in 2013).

So obviously they have met the challenge of omni-channel retail. The question is, how did they do it?

In 2007, Home Depot's direct-to-store distribution model was very decentralized. Each store handled the ordering, replenishing, and managing of inventory, requiring up to 60 percent of store labor, taking time away from customers.

APPROACH

While digital sales is the fastest growing part of Home Depot's (HD) business, 40 percent of the sales have been fulfilled by their "brick-and-mortar" stores, making this really an omni-channel success story.

Home Depot's current omni-channel fulfillment options are: "buy online pickup in-store" (BOPIS), "buy online return to store" (BORIS), "buy online ship to store" (BOSS), and "buy online deliver from store" (BODFS), a new option which enables them to fulfill online orders directly from stores with next-day delivery within a two-hour delivery window.

Building a distribution network that can deliver on the question "do you want to pick up your order at the store or have it delivered to your home?" for every customer every time has not been simple to achieve.

HD has restructured its supply network to integrate the experiences of in-store and online commerce, recognizing the customer value of online inventory visibility and product research, and transforming its online store to meet these needs.

Most important, however, is the fact that HD has implemented an integrated network of distribution centers that furnishes both direct-to-customer fulfillment orders and store replenishment, and of course also manages the "buy online, pickup in-store" and "buy online, deliver from store" methods as well.

To accomplish this, they built a series of rapid deployment centers (RDCs). Suppliers and vendors no longer ship thousands of orders to Home Depot stores, but create orders bound for 18 North American RDCs that ship items through the rest of the company's network.

Upon arrival at the RDC, product might be cross-docked and allocated to stores based on real-time demand. They also developed three direct fulfillment centers (DFCs) to take on faster-moving SKUs that were shipping vendor-direct in addition to a longer tail of slower-moving SKUs as merchants complement in-store inventory with a more diverse range online.

The new DFCs leverage store inventory with omni-channel algorithms to greatly improve the speed of delivery or pickup of goods based on the customer needs in an interconnected environment.

RESULTS

The results speak for themselves as mentioned previously. However, their future plans are not to build new U.S. stores. Instead, HD likes to think of all of its transaction processes as fulfillment, no matter how the goods get to the customer. So instead, in the U.S., future investments are being made in existing stores in order to double them up as fulfillment centers to drive further omni-channel sales.

The three direct fulfillment centers (DFCs) mentioned previously have improved shipping speeds and are now able to guarantee two-day parcel delivery to 90 percent of the U.S. population.

Ultimately, their vision is to have physical assets and new virtual assets come together to enhance the customer experience, resulting in interconnected retail (Figure 8.3) [Waldron, 2019].

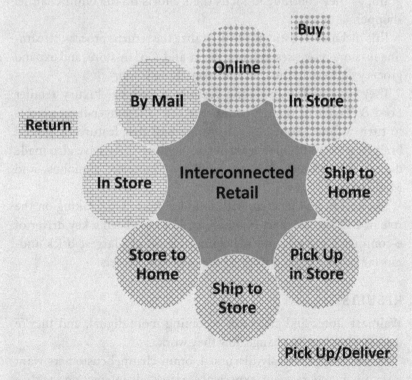

FIGURE 8.3
Home Depot interconnected retail.

CASE STUDY #2: WALMART, AN EARLY LEADER IN OMNI-CHANNEL STRATEGIES

CHALLENGE

The recent challenge for Walmart, the large mass merchandiser, is to continue to build its e-commerce business while at the same time staying competitive with e-commerce giant Amazon, and not damaging profitability. This is especially important to Walmart as they have observed that people who shop across channels are extremely important to them as they spend twice as much as those who only shop in-store.

APPROACH

Walmart has spent $1.2 billion recently on its e-commerce program, as they continue to focus their efforts on the omni-channel shopper.

This includes investments to digitalize the returns process, streamline in-store processes, roll out "Scan-and-Go" in-store, and expand grocery delivery in the U.S. and around the world.

They have added an online version of designer luxury retailer Lord & Taylor to their e-commerce site. The longer-term plan is to turn walmart.com into an online mall that features high-end brands, with additional deals in the pipeline. They have also made digital acquisitions such as ShoeBuy, Moosejaw, Bonobos, and ModCloth.

The deal to buy Jet.com, with founder, Marc Lore, taking on the role of CEO at Walmart eCommerce U.S., has been a key driver of e-commerce growth and is helping the world's largest brick-and-mortar retailer expand its presence in urban markets.

RESULTS

Walmart stores and clubs are becoming more digital, and they're using technology to change how they work.

As we have previously discussed, omni-channel customers want a seamless and relevant experience across all interactions with a brand, and by having customer analytics capabilities, Walmart is able to translate that information into actionable insights.

Lore and other Walmart leaders are trying to reinvent everything from in-store pickup to how customers shop for groceries. For example, they offer grocery pickup at more than 2,100 locations and grocery delivery at nearly 800 locations.

Walmart is using retail technology to break the barriers between digital and physical realities, and so far, it seems successful, as e-commerce sales increased 23 percent for the fourth quarter of 2018 and 44 percent for the full year [Thompson, 2018].

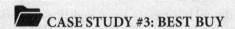 **CASE STUDY #3: BEST BUY**

CHALLENGE

Best Buy was on a roll after it vanquished its rival, Circuit City, and was selling more electronics per square foot than any other retailer. But by 2012 business was down as the tough economy had not been kind to their bottom line, with profits in the second quarter of 2012 down 91 percent from the same period in 2011 while the company's share price had fallen 60 percent over the previous two years.

They had an even bigger challenge at that point as the entire big-box retail industry appeared to be dying, with more curated shopping, like at the Apple store which has a more limited assortment of hardware, software, and accessories, making it easier for sales people to answer customers' questions.

E-commerce had created "showrooming" where customers came to the store to get hands-on experience with a product, and then used their smartphone to purchase it from Amazon at a lower price.

Furthermore, new sites were transforming consumer behavior. For example, Etsy and Kickstarter turned tech gear and accessories from commodities into vehicles for individual expression (i.e. what is known as "mass customization"). Best Buy had profitably grown through selling mass tech products by stocking large amounts of inventory in its huge showrooms.

Now, it couldn't always offer the best prices, its stores didn't carry many of the latest gadgets, and its employees often couldn't answer some basic questions.

APPROACH

To deal with these challenges, it brought in a new CEO, Hubert Joly, along with a new executive team. While they did close 50 stores, they realized that they needed to turn the real estate into an advantage as they had long-term leases and wouldn't really be able to sell the stores to another big-box retailer. So, they decided to focus on the strengths of physical retail that online companies simply can't match, such as the fact that people want to try before they buy, which they can't do on Amazon.

Also, BestBuy.com was the 11th-largest e-commerce site, booking about $3 billion a year and growing by 15 to 20 percent every quarter.

Behind that digital business is a vast logistics network that delivers products quickly and reliably to 1,400 stores across the country.

So, they had the digital and physical assets, but they just needed to figure out how to use them more effectively.

They launched a pilot project in 50 stores. When a customer comes in to test out a few high-end cameras, a sales rep with a tablet can meet them to compare specs on the various models. The rep can pull up a list of comparison sites to locate the lowest price and match it. If the product isn't in stock, the rep can help them place an order through BestBuy.com. The customer has a choice of delivery methods, same-day in-store pickup or home delivery (which can include an in-home photo-editing tutorial). Almost half of Best Buy's online customers have their purchases delivered to the store, not their home, mainly because it's faster and many don't want expensive electronics left outside their homes and also may have questions about setup, features, and accessories.

Ultimately, Best Buy is trying to be all things to all shoppers, which is not an easy task. They want to be a high-end customer-service experience, similar to the Apple Store, and an infinite online warehouse that can compete on price with the likes of Amazon, combining mass-market and niche.

RESULTS

Fast forward to 2018 where Best Buy saw its online sales increase 12 percent to $1.14 billion in the first quarter, representing 13.6 percent of total revenue, up from 12.9 percent the previous year. Overall company revenue increased 6.8 percent in Q1 to $9.1 billion, with same-store sales up a healthy 7.1 percent. This was helped by the company's continued omni-channel investments, improved inventory management, and ongoing supply chain transformation.

They have seen their customers shopping in multiple channels as well as material increases in the number of customers choosing to pick up their online orders in stores.

They have seen a reduction in "at-risk inventory" across channels as customers are consistently telling them that the reason for an improved customer experience year-over-year is inventory availability both online and in stores, as very few customers shop in just one channel.

They have increased investment in automation and more local distribution capabilities for online orders, expanded the space (for online order fulfillment), and improved the customer experience while growing the sales of large products that must be delivered.

Best Buy has also created a business unit last summer to focus on developing sales of consumer electronics into the secondary markets, opening a new era of reverse logistics. No longer were the handling of customer returns, returns to vendor, and overstock a cost center sitting in a corner somewhere, but instead they were transformed into a profit center.

To accomplish this, they had to create partnerships with customers, manufacturers, and third-party service providers. The goal is for Best Buy to move towards providing its customers full lifecycle management of the products it sells, and for its vendors, partnerships that focus on lifecycle profitability [Copeland, 2012].

Successfully meeting all of the challenges omni-channel retail creates requires the development of an aligned omni-channel supply chain strategy which includes selecting the right people, processes, and technologies to successfully navigate industry-specific challenges and opportunities. This is the topic of our next chapter.

Part IV

Transformational Omni-Channel Supply Chain Strategies to Achieve a Competitive Advantage

9

Omni-Channel Supply Chain Strategy: E-Commerce and Brick-and-Mortar Combined

WHAT IS A SUPPLY CHAIN STRATEGY?

In general, a supply chain strategy can be defined as *a formal written plan that details what actions the organization is going to take over a multi-year horizon.*

A supply chain strategy therefore, is extremely important (and not always formulated, at up to 80 percent of companies in some surveys), as the supply chain can account for 60–80 percent of a company's total revenue, which is a large number that deserves detailed, multi-year planning.

Secondly, an organization's supply chain usually operates as a service or support organization for the rest of the company. A strategic plan can help the company's functions and executives to accept and support supply chain-aligned strategies. An example would be to roll out S&OP capabilities across the globe over a multi-year span.

The strategy can be the key tool that helps keep the supply aligned with the overall business strategy (Figure 9.1). If, for example, the company employs a "response" strategy, then the supply chain must be lean and agile for the company strategy to be successful.

Dittmann suggested a nine-step plan for building a supply chain:

1. Start with customers' current and future needs (as discussed above).
2. Assess current supply chain capabilities relative to best in class.
3. Evaluate supply chain "game changers" (what megatrends will impact customers and the supply chain?).

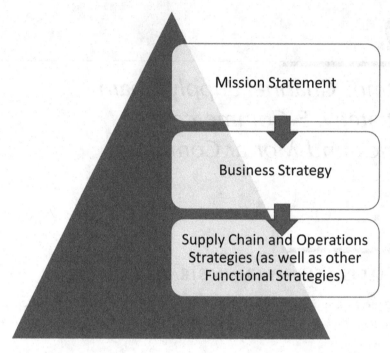

FIGURE 9.1
Business and supply chain strategy alignment.

4. Analyze the competition (something too few do for sure).
5. Survey technology – What is new or coming out there?
6. Deal with supply chain risk – Risk management needs to be part of the strategy document.
7. Develop new supply chain capability requirements and create a plan to get there.
8. Evaluate current supply chain organizational structure, people, and metrics.
9. Develop a business case and get buy-in [Gilmore, 2013].

SOME OMNI-CHANNEL SUPPLY CHAIN STRATEGY OPTIONS

Lean, agile supply chains are needed to help retailers gain access to the omni-channel growth opportunity and to profitably compete across channels with the right mix of product, price, and service. To have a chance of being successful, supply chain management needs to be elevated to a higher level in the organization. After that, change management is needed for executive buy-in to the expanded role of SCM. Finally, strategies (and execution) for the better alignment of inventory with demand and high fulfillment velocity and value to the customer are required.

The 6th Annual State of the Retail Supply Chain Report (2016) surveyed members and readers and found the following strategic options:

Drive company growth through SCM – E-commerce, while a small (7.5 percent) part of retail sales, is where most of the growth in retail can be found. So there has been a shift away from logistics-cost optimization to customer-value creation, with the goal of driving sales.

As a result, current supply chain processes, metrics, and incentives must be recalibrated to promote growth and customer service. At the same time, customer choice creates supply chain complexity. Retailers now need customer-centric supply chains that can consistently serve demand from virtually anywhere in the network, while not significantly reducing profit margins.

Support effective changes required of omni-channel supply chain management – To successfully serve omni-channel demand, an integrated agile network of resources and processes must replace the traditional sequential activities and flows, requiring vast changes.

Many retailers have made the more gradual transition from the use of third-party fulfillment for their online business, to handling online fulfillment internally in dedicated e-commerce facilities, to eventually moving toward a unified internal process that integrates the fulfillment of online orders with store-based processes, while others may choose a more direct change approach. No matter, either transition also requires significant upgrades to technology and logistics processes.

Retailers must go beyond the alignment of demand planning, inventory management, order fulfillment, store replenishment, and returns management with more extensive engagement between the supply chain organization and other retail entities. Four examples of changes are:

1. Supply chain and store leadership collaborating to establish store-based fulfillment capabilities.
2. The building of cross-functional store teams to support omni-channel efforts.

3. Some leading retailers in the study are either moving demand-planning activities completely into the supply chain area, or are embedding supply chain staff in the merchant group to improve forecasting and allocation.

4. Omni-channel retailers are working more closely with both vendors and carriers. With today's "endless aisle" giving access to a brand's full catalog of SKUs through in-store kiosks, mobile devices, and websites that link to retailer and vendor stock across the supply chain, vendors become an extension of the retail enterprise and need to meet the commitments the retailer has made to its customers. The same is true of parcel carriers, requiring carriers and retailers to work much more closely together, as carriers are now a "proxy" of retailer excellence.

These changes to processes and relationships must be properly planned out, communicated, and supported to gain "buy-in" and better chances for success.

Align inventory with demand – Omni-channel complicates the always important strategy (and task) of getting inventory into the right place, as you need to fill omni-channel orders quickly while still trying to fill the order as efficiently as possible from the best (i.e. low-cost) location.

More powerful order management systems are necessary to coordinate inventory, order status, and location with customer demand since information such as order origination point, customer (consumer) contact information, and delivery addresses are now also needed.

There are multiple strategies for achieving this. One is to establish highly detailed demand plans; another is to view inventory as a singular enterprise resource that can be accessed to meet demand from any channel by linking inventory across the entire network to function as a single pool of inventory that is available to support multiple demand streams.

This needs to be supported by agile fulfillment which constantly reviews and allocates inventory across the network, on an individual order basis, to fill online demand efficiently and cost-effectively.

The option of purchasing items online and selecting home delivery or store pickup further complicates things. Some retailers are placing more emphasis on centralizing orders (and inventories), while others are trying to push many e-commerce orders to stores.

Improve omni-channel velocity and value – Ultimately, omni-channel retailers try to move product more quickly to the point of sale, in many cases in small quantities, all the while keeping logistics costs under control.

Traditionally, brick-and-mortar retail strove for high on-shelf availability driving the development of high-volume, case-pick distribution centers and truckload deliveries to stores. While this still exists, supply chains have to adapt to the realities of omni-channel retailing where mobile apps and websites allow customers to order product from anywhere for delivery to anywhere in small quantities at customer-defined transit times.

While this is similar to catalog shopping, which has been around for over 100 years (you would think Sears would have been more successful in e-commerce!), omni-channel has greatly expanded the number of orders and participants, not to mention the speed and efficiency of fulfillment. More "mom-and-pop" type retailers have outsourced this process to 3PLs, and larger retailers have invested in dedicated e-commerce fulfillment centers to accommodate their volume and expand their online offerings.

Another strategic option is to establish integrated fulfillment centers that support both store replenishment and e-commerce orders, leveraging the same inventory for both demand streams and avoiding facility duplication.

Today, many retailers are also moving to in-store fulfillment. Delivery costs can be reduced with local delivery or eliminated with store pickup. The hard part is to perform fulfillment operations without too rapidly depleting inventory levels also needed for in-store demand. One solution would be to have more frequent store replenishment. Another would be to employ a "hub store" concept where a single store acts as a fulfillment center for a high-population region, which would minimize disruption at other stores in the area.

It should be noted that most State of the Retail Supply Chain survey respondents used multiple fulfillment strategies to meet speed and cost goals.

In the end, there may be no single fulfillment strategy that is best for all retailers. Strategy selection should be based on the ability to meet service commitments and maintain fulfillment costs for a given set of customer order characteristics [Ishfaq, Gibson, and Defee, 2016].

ARE YOU READY FOR OMNI-CHANNEL RETAIL?

As stated a number of times in this book, an omni-channel retail strategy provides a consistent shopping experience across different channels and devices, requiring your supply chain to offer a smooth, positive experience for customers – no matter where or how they interact with your brand.

Some supply chain challenges to address when dealing with an omni-channel retail strategy include:

Supply chain visibility – Consumer expectations are increasing, and supply chains are extending. You need timely and accurate inventory information for all parts of the supply chain, whether physically integrated or separate – for example, distribution centers to support stores and fulfillment centers for e-commerce.

Use technologies such as RFID, barcodes, the Internet of things (IoT), blockchain, and the cloud to track inventory in the warehouse, the store, or in transit.

Network design – Design the network appropriately for rapid delivery, free or low-cost shipping, and free returns, and determine optimal inventory placement.

Consider segmenting the supply chain to achieve optimal stocking and delivery performance, while maintaining low operation costs, by grouping products with shared stocking, delivery, and fulfillment needs. This may require different supply chain strategies; for example, should you integrate distribution and fulfillment center processes at some echelons of the distribution network and separate them at others?

Order fulfillment – Omni-channel retail creates a range of customer touchpoints – stores, outlets, e-commerce sites, catalogs, and seasonal pop-up locations. This means the supply chain also gains additional responsibilities similar to sales associates and merchandising managers.

Then there is the increased demand – and added complexity – for ship-to-store and ship-from-store delivery, turning retail locations into mini-fulfillment centers requiring picking, packing, and possibly delivery capabilities.

When operating a multi-channel distribution center, the picking process is more complex, making it critical to keep costs down. Automated picking systems and voice-assisted picking can help in this regard.

Additionally, pick and pack robots can communicate with other information systems and put together the pieces for an order, and voice-assisted picking software can allow warehouse employees to receive direction from automated systems to help pick an order, increasing the speed and accuracy of orders leaving the warehouse.

Pricing – Determine if pricing will be channel-specific, a single omni-channel price, or some combination, as many consumers use smartphones in the store to compare prices – and use online coupons – before purchasing. The price can help determine if consumers want items delivered to their homes or if they want to pick them up at the nearest store.

Customer service – Omni-channel retail expands the customer experience beyond the store. Many stores contact customers through social media, live chat, or text messaging, so employees need to be trained correctly when they are contacted through any channel.

Consider using CRM systems to keep detailed customer profiles and document interactions, so that anyone who deals with that customer will already have their information, which helps reduce customer frustration.

Reverse logistics – A convenient returns policy and process are essential to the customer experience, so make returns convenient through in-store, prepaid mail, and drop point channels.

Develop a strategy that includes omni-channel return options, where all designated return locations have the proper tools and information to determine quick and accurate product disposition.

Customer engagement – The service received by the customer directly impacts their buying decision, longer term commitment to the brand, and their likelihood of recommending the product.

Additionally, the increased use of social media and communication channels has created new points of contact with customers, and organizations must meet and engage them on their terms to provide a quality experience.

Retailers are constantly working to develop omni-channel strategies for their customers, and it is important that "best in class" retailers not end up with separate customer experiences online and in-store.

Companies need to provide an experience that will build a strong long-term relationship, with loyalty programs designed to encourage and reward customers who purchase regularly from a retailer.

These are some of the major challenges that supply chain executives will meet along the way towards supporting omni-channel retail. They should be considered early on in your journey as it's always better to be part of the solution rather than part of the problem [Myerson, 2018a].

OMNI-CHANNEL RETAIL: FOUR RULES FOR SUCCESS

While it's not possible to be truly omniscient when it comes to omni-channel retail and your supply chain, it is possible to try to anticipate some of the challenges ahead as part of your organization's strategy.

Omni-channel decision-makers anticipate disruptions led by drones, autonomous vehicles, and crowdsourced delivery, a recent Zebra Technologies study found.

Survey results indicate that in response to today's consumer, who expects an integrated, faster purchasing transaction, and the growth of e-commerce, 78 percent of logistics companies expect to provide same-day delivery by 2023 and 40 percent anticipate delivery within a two-hour window by 2028.

To successfully navigate these "white-water rapids", a metaphor describing how managers navigate change where the organization is a small raft navigating a raging river, companies will have to select winning processes and technologies and not wait until the last minute. So, in a way, they need to be somewhat omniscient.

A Bain & Company white paper titled "Modern Retail Supply Chains: Backbone for Omni-Channel" points out the following four basic rules for success to consider when adapting to the new and evolving reality of omni-channel retail:

1. Understand your business and customer strategy – Learn as much as you can about your customers, including how they shop, how they want to receive and return goods, and what they will pay for. Understanding these strategies can help you avoid unnecessary changes and investments that can disrupt your supply chain and harm your bottom line.

2. Develop capabilities to support your strategy – Customize services to meet customer needs. For example, do they desire same-day delivery? Do they buy online and pick up in-store? Developing these capabilities involves decisions such as whether to insource or outsource activities including e-commerce fulfillment, transportation, and returns and how to integrate these and other processes with the rest of your supply chain.

3. Adapt your operating model – Take a 360 view and involve other functions such as marketing, merchandising, e-commerce, store management, and IT in supply chain decisions. There are plenty of trade-offs in operating decisions such as cost vs. service (for example, transportation costs vs. same-day delivery), so these decisions should be as collaborative as possible to ensure that there is buy-in and that success is measured properly.

4. Invest in technology and analytics – Improve technology throughout the supply chain to help with all kinds of processes, from forecasting and customer order tracking to reordering quantities and restocking locations. By linking these decisions with your strategy, you can avoid a lot of unnecessary investments because it can be tempting to jump on the latest technology without first doing your due diligence.

Starting with these four rules should lead you down the right path to make positive changes to people, processes, and technologies in your supply chain [Myerson, 2019b].

Successfully aligning inventory management, order fulfillment, delivery, and returns with customer demands in an omni-channel environment requires agility and flexibility across the entire supply chain. Supply chain executives must constantly rethink their supply chain design in the next five years because of this emerging cross-channel fulfillment. That is the topic of our next chapter.

10

Impact of Omni-Channel Retail on the Supply Chain Network

SUPPLY CHAINS MUST ADAPT TO OMNI-CHANNEL RETAIL

While omni-channel retail has rapidly become a source of growth in consumer goods and retail, few companies are confident about their ability to execute it and maintain margins.

Omni-channel has placed the supply chain front and center, with consumers expecting to shop, purchase, and return goods across a variety of channels, and the supply chain reaching beyond the retail store to the consumer's home and dedicated pickup points. This requires real-time visibility of inventory across the supply chain and a single view of the consumer as they move from one channel to another.

The growing number of channels has increased the complexity especially from a logistics point of view. The fulfillment process is more complicated, because brick-and-mortar retailing is increasingly overlapping with distance e-commerce retail. Before, supply chain management was responsible for delivering goods to a retail store only, as the store was the end point of the transaction. Online retailing has now placed distribution systems at the forefront, since retailers need to offer a variety of options for finding, buying, and returning goods across brick-and-mortar stores and websites. Brick-and-mortar stores today are only one of multiple channels. With the new set of channels, retailers must simultaneously accommodate and anticipate demand and ensure availability, meet varying lead times, and keep costs down for each channel.

An EY survey determined that omni-channel is a critical driver for growth for the consumer goods and retail industry, but that the traditional consumer goods supply chain is not fit for purpose and must be re-engineered

The survey concluded that to remain profitable, companies need to embed an omni-channel supply chain into their business strategy, with a goal of transforming their supply chain to be truly agile and responsive, with robust data analytics capabilities.

While there are many benefits of omni-channel such as improved consumer insight, strengthened consumer loyalty, and competitive differentiation, omni-channel has become a drag on many companies' profits as many have rushed into it, often bolting on systems and processes without fully considering integration with traditional store fulfillment. As a result, supply chains are inefficient and there is a lack of visibility across different channels.

Respondents from the survey found the following reasons or barriers to maximizing omni-channel benefit in the supply chain:

1. Lack of dedicated resources and capabilities
2. Level of investment required to succeed
3. Challenge of supply chain complexity
4. Limitations of siloed organizational structures
5. Lack of senior leadership support

The primary reason for many of these barriers is that most consumer goods supply chains were traditionally seen as a cost center to deliver goods to stores. But, in an omni-channel world, the supply chain is a consumer-facing front office and ultimately decides if shoppers have a good or bad experience.

The key enablers to be successful with an omni-channel strategy is to have:

- Omni-channel embedded in the overall company strategy.
- A responsive, combined omni and traditional supply chain infrastructure.
- IT systems and capabilities that enable seamless visibility and fulfillment for end consumers.

What Needs to Be Done?

Companies can no longer create strategies in silos or bolt on new channels without integrating them. To succeed, companies must embrace omni-channel and ensure that it is fully embedded in their overall corporate strategy and organizational culture (Figure 10.1).

They must start with understanding what consumers want and how their needs and expectations are changing.

Existing channel silos must be modified, key performance indicators (KPIs) replaced, and new processes and technologies implemented.

Everything must be looked at through an omni-channel view, from the product and packaging design, to promotional planning, operating model design, and supply chain.

Omni-channel challenges the singular focus on efficiency and requires a new level of responsiveness. A segmented supply chain and inventory model will help to strike the balance between agility and efficiency.

In omni-channel, deciding on what inventory to stock where becomes more complex. Companies must now make decisions about the level of stock that is sent to stores vs. being held back for online availability.

Finally, omni-channel is increasing supply chain complexity. The mix continues to shift, with emerging channels, like "click and collect" which is a hybrid e-commerce model in which people purchase or select items

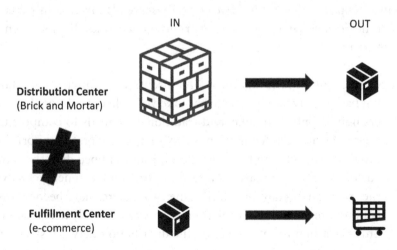

FIGURE 10.1
Distribution vs. fulfillment centers.

online and pick them up in-store or at a centralized collection point, and which is growing in popularity. Companies will need to adapt their supply chain infrastructure to keep pace with these trends, ensuring that they have the agility to respond to highly complex consumer behavior without a negative impact on profits [EY.com, 2015b].

DISTRIBUTION DISRUPTION: READY OR NOT, HERE IT COMES

Disruptive changes in distribution networks are dramatically reshaping current logistics models.

Sometimes it seems like things are changing so fast that we can hardly keep up with what's going on around us in the world. For example, doesn't it seem like smartphones and their current operating systems become "old" almost overnight? Can you imagine the impact of these constant changes on one's supply chain? Well, if you can't imagine it, you may be in trouble.

Chris Caplice, executive director of MIT's Center for Transportation and Logistics, identifies "Four Trends That Could Redefine Distribution in the U.S." to help us organize our thoughts on the subject so that we can try to anticipate some of this. If we don't, these trends can certainly create lots of inefficiencies in our current distribution networks. The four trends to consider are:

Diversification of sales channels – As discussed, omni-channel retailing has grown as e-commerce has taken off, where traditional retailers bundle online, mobile, and traditional channels to compete for sales. This has resulted in omni-channel distribution to support this process. Products can be ordered online and shipped directly to the customer or in some cases "shipped to store" for customer pickup vs. the traditional retail model. In some cases, stores have become distribution centers to supply e-commerce orders directly to customers. This has a significant impact on the distribution network structure and capacity.

Densification of products – Back in the early 1990s household products companies transitioned to concentrated "ultra" laundry detergents, while portable computer storage has gone from floppy disks to thumbnail drives. This evolution has enabled companies to reduce the number of containers, trucks, and railcars used in distribution networks and in some cases, potentially shift to other, faster modes such as air.

Decentralization of production – In the past, economies of scale were key, where massive manufacturing plants supplied your entire customer base. Now, with the global economy, and improvements in technology and processes, production can be decentralized into smaller, regionally based manufacturing facilities (owned or subcontracted) closer to population centers. This has had a significant impact on transportation and shipping patterns as well as lead times.

Digitalization of products – There has been a long trend of movement from physical to information-based products, and not just books, music, and movies, as it is now starting to happen to more traditional products. Think of the potential impact on Crayola from their "Color Alive" line of products, where a special app and crayon transform coloring by activating a virtual experience complete with color effects. This could drastically reshape their distribution needs as there comes more of a reliance on digital technology and less on physical crayons.

So, the disruption from these types of changes to our distribution networks and entire supply chains will dramatically reshape our current logistics models. The real question is: Will you be ready for them [Myerson, 2016a]?

OMNI-CHANNEL MULTIPLIES THE CHALLENGES FOR DISTRIBUTION-CENTRIC SUPPLY CHAINS

Companies have some big decisions to make about when and how to invest in realigning their supply chains to accommodate an omni-channel pipeline.

When e-commerce first emerged, most retailers were able to use a small section of an existing distribution center to fulfill online orders. As demand grew, many retailers opened fulfillment centers dedicated to picking and packing individual orders.

To clarify, a distribution center traditionally ships orders in bulk to retailers or wholesalers, while fulfillment centers are designed for packing single orders shipped to an individual end user. On the surface, each has a very different type of operation (and cost structure) from the other, as a distribution center typically handles pallet and case quantities, and a fulfillment center handles individual piece pick and small parcel orders.

As we know, the goal of an omni-channel retail approach is to integrate all of a retailer's channels, creating a seamless shopping experience no matter how the shopper is accessing the product.

So as a result of an omni-channel strategy, some retailers, such as Gap, American Eagle, and now Target, are experimenting with consolidating their distribution and fulfillment centers into one facility, often requiring a new warehouse management system (and material handling systems) intended to better integrate their distribution and fulfillment operations.

In Target's case at a test facility in Perth Amboy, NJ, their goal is to take their replenishment cycle from days to hours and reduce inventory at stores. This requires sending shipments to stores more frequently and in smaller lots to more precisely meet demand, rather than shipping big cases of products, allowing Target to expand its use of stores to fulfill online orders with less inventory held at stores, dedicating more room to digital fulfillment.

Before embarking on such a strategy, one must consider the advantages of traditional separated facilities vs. combined omni-channel systems. Some of the advantages of combined facilities include potentially lower operational costs, as fewer facilities generally equate to lower duplication and therefore lower operating costs, shared inventory, and more immediate control and flexibility.

On the other hand, there are many advantages of having separate facilities, such as lower capital costs since a new shared infrastructure requires significant investment, having more options when dealing with order fulfillment challenges, and the fact that omni-channel facilities handle a lot more SKUs than brick-and-mortar retail locations, giving the potential to run out of space due to future rapid growth in omni-channel retail.

Obviously, there's a lot to consider here before making such a huge, long-term strategic decision, but it is one that will have to be made at some point in the near future [Myerson, 2018a].

STORE DELIVERY KEEPS RETAILERS IN THE GAME

Multi-channel retail and fulfillment are typically based on the assumption that customers choose a main way to connect, whether through physical stores or a website. Many retailers manage each channel separately with different teams, budgets, processes, tools, reporting structures, and revenue goals.

In multi-channel retail and fulfillment, stores have their own stock and sell directly to customers, while the website has its own separate stock. Customers purchasing items in stores can make returns only in-store and often can't return online orders in-store. Customers' online interactions with the retailer are completely separated from offline interactions.

In an omni-channel environment, however, consumers are likely to have multiple touchpoints with a retailer and expect their interactions between each channel to be seamless. Customers can order what they want, when they want, on whatever device they want, and have it delivered how they want.

A key difference between multi-channel and omni-channel is that omni-channel joins the touchpoints together so that, whatever method or combination of methods the customer chooses to make a purchase, their experience is consistent, seamless, and unified. But omni-channel fulfillment can be tricky. Some companies sell online only, while others have brick-and-mortar stores and add an online channel. Still others started off as online-only companies but are adding some form of showroom-only storefront or pop-up store.

Omni-channel customers buying online may take delivery in a variety of forms from one order to the next, in addition to traditional visits to a retail location. Furthermore, e-commerce has complicated the last mile of delivery, making it more difficult for traditional retailers.

Getting Creative

Traditional last-mile delivery involves many challenges, including cost minimization, transparency, and efficiency. Those challenges, along with the growth of e-commerce, are forcing brick-and-mortar retailers to become more creative (Figure 10.2).

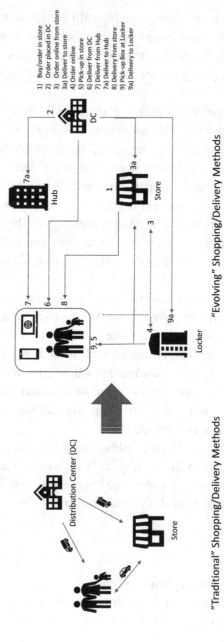

1) Buy/order in store
2) Order placed in DC
3) Order online from store
3a) Deliver to store
4) Order online
5) Pick-up in store
6) Deliver from DC
7) Deliver from Hub
7a) Deliver to Hub
8) Delivery from store
9) Pick-up Box at Locker
9a) Delivery to Locker

"Evolving" Shopping/Delivery Methods

"Traditional" Shopping/Delivery Methods

FIGURE 10.2
Evolution of shopping/delivery methods.

E-commerce businesses such as Amazon have been exploring air and land drone delivery and lockers in pre-designated locations available for customer pickup, among other innovative methods.

Some large retailers such as Walmart and Best Buy are using their stores as distribution centers where employees pick items from the shelves and backrooms to fulfill online orders. They either load the orders into FedEx or UPS trucks, or, as Walmart is testing, deliver packages themselves on their way home.

Stores can potentially cut costs substantially by having employees pick and deliver from stores, as last-mile delivery costs are a significant part of fulfillment costs. Furthermore, in the case of Walmart, two-thirds of the U.S. population live within five miles of a store.

Additional benefits of store last-mile delivery include switching online orders to locations with the most inventory of an item, reducing the need for discounts, and fulfilling orders for items that are out of stock at e-commerce fulfillment centers.

By enabling store delivery, traditional retailers may have found a better way to compete with Amazon's fulfillment network of 100+ distribution centers: Using their hundreds, or thousands, of brick-and-mortar locations as DCs [Myerson, 2018b].

E-Commerce Looking for Room to Grow

Many activities that were typically carried out within stores are now consolidated into logistics facilities with the advent of e-commerce and omni-channel retail, which is also driving the industrial real estate market as discussed in Chapter 7.

We've all heard about recent retail store closings at successful companies such as Kohl's, Macy's, and Walmart. A major reason for this is the shift from brick-and-mortar stores to the growth of e-commerce as a result of omni-channel marketing and distribution. This of course has a huge impact on the retail supply chain network.

In fact, according to an NFI Industries article, entitled "The E-Commerce Effect on the Commercial Real Estate Industry",

> In 2014, e-commerce sales for United States retailers surpassed $300 billion for the first time, reaching $304.9 billion, which was a 15.4% increase in comparison to the previous year and is the fifth year in a row that web

sales growth has been close to or above 15%. As companies are increasingly offering same-day delivery, gift wrapping, ship-to-store and other e-commerce advantages, consumers are opting to do more of their shopping online.

As e-commerce continues to grow, industries like commercial real estate are adapting to offer more ideal solutions to support e-commerce goals. E-commerce has shifted what companies look for in their real estate facilities and has evolved what is now expected in today's fulfillment centers [Myerson, 2016a].

After considering the impact of omni-channel retail on your supply chain network, you need to next look at the actual fulfillment operations, which are a lot different from traditional brick-and-mortar distribution methods.

11

Impact of Omni-Channel Retail on Fulfillment Operations

Fulfillment for e-commerce orders is a different "animal" than traditional brick-and-mortar distribution as e-commerce orders typically are smaller than those for traditional brick-and-mortar distribution centers, and often require one-day fulfillment.

When the two methods are combined, omni-channel retail creates a range of customer touchpoints – stores, outlets, e-commerce sites, catalogs, and seasonal pop-up locations. This means the supply chain also gains additional responsibilities similar to sales associates and merchandising managers.

On top of that, there is the increased demand for – and added complexity of – ship-to-store and ship-from-store delivery, turning retail locations into mini-fulfillment centers requiring picking, packing, and possibly delivery capabilities.

WHAT IS OMNI-CHANNEL FULFILLMENT?

Order fulfillment, in general, is the complete process involved in receiving, processing, and delivering orders to end customers.

In traditional brick-and-mortar store fulfillment, merchandise is shipped, usually in lot-sized quantities (i.e. pallets, cases, racks, etc.) to the stores using some blend of push and demand-driven pull replenishment.

On the other hand, on a high level, omni-channel fulfillment is the order fulfillment process across multiple channels.

The most common fulfillment model is a straight "order in-warehouse fulfills" process. This does not always leverage the retailer's full resources as it may not always be the best option for the merchant. Omni-channel fulfillment is about choosing the option that makes the most sense for that order.

As discussed earlier, there are a variety of ways to fulfill omni-channel orders including ship-from-DC, ship-from-3PL (or manufacturer), ship-from-store, ship-to-store (for in-store pickup), and ship-to-partner (pickup depot/carrier/locker).

Using agreed-upon business rules within the order management system, management can determine which method is appropriate on a case-by-case basis.

ADVANTAGES OF OMNI-CHANNEL FULFILLMENT STRATEGY

This gives retailers using omni-channel fulfillment some distinct advantages such as:

- Gives the retailer a lever to run the business – They can choose from a variety of methods by focusing on cost, speed, or efficiency (e.g. shipping the entire order in one consolidated box) of the selected fulfillment method.
- Customer satisfaction – The fulfillment methods mentioned above, and others, can be varied based upon customer wants and desires. For example, if the retailer promise to the customer is to reduce their carbon footprint, consolidating all online orders into one box from the closest location to the customer may be a priority.
- A responsive, agile supply chain – If there are several options to deliver goods to shoppers, when one fulfillment route fails, the operation can shift to one or more of the other options, whereas retailers that only use the ship-from-DC option have no flexibility. For example, during a severe winter snow storm, a retailer using omni-channel fulfillment can quickly change business rules by changing the fulfillment center from a snowed-in DC to stores not affected by the storm who can ship the orders themselves [Dimov, 2018].

CHALLENGES WITH OMNI-CHANNEL FULFILLMENT STRATEGY

Omni-channel allows retailers to meet customer expectations, but there are also some challenges to consider when pursuing an omni-channel fulfillment strategy. Some of the main challenges include:

Inventory visibility across all channels – Most retailers already fulfill orders through a multi-channel mix of in-store fulfillment and direct-to-consumer fulfillment of e-commerce orders. However, an omni-channel fulfillment strategy complicates things by offering alternative methods of fulfilling orders, such as buy online, pick up in-store (BOPS) and/or last-mile fulfillment from stores. Therefore, clear inventory visibility becomes even more important in an omni-channel fulfillment strategy as the various new channels can make it even harder for an operation to view accurate, real-time inventory availability, which can thus lead to difficulty in demand planning and inventory optimization.

Dissimilar orders should be picked from the same inventory, at the same time – The mechanics of fulfillment are greatly affected by an omni-channel strategy. While it will be dependent on the exact operation, you may have a variety of order types including:

- Wholesale orders – Typically picked in larger quantities (i.e. full case, split case, or pallet).
- Retail orders – Typically picked in full or split cases.
- E-commerce orders – Average two line items per order.

If these are picked from a single inventory with a single material handling system, you need to have the optimal strategies, processes, and technologies to be successful.

Multiple channels must be combined into a unified brand experience – While omni-channel fulfillment is complex, it is also challenging to present a unified experience on the customer end, so retailers need to make it as easy for customers to move between the various channels as possible. Brick-and-mortar, e-commerce, and apps should feel connected, not unconnected, as customers move between the channels in order to provide a brand experience that builds customer affinity, encouraging them to return [Ziegler, 2018].

E-COMMERCE IMPACT ON WAREHOUSE OPERATIONS

Fulfillment requirements, due to the rapid growth of e-commerce as well as a greater focus on leaning out the supply chain, have had a great impact on warehouse operations with far fewer full pallets and cases being picked and more individual items.

Supply chain executives need to rethink fulfillment processes, technology needs, operational priorities, and warehouse footprints, as well as the roles of value-chain partnerships.

An ARC Advisory Group and DC Velocity magazine survey about facilities, market pressures, operations, and investment priorities found the following:

1) **DCs' Changing Footprint**

   On average, respondents' facility footprints are almost half bulk warehousing (facilities with more than 100,000 square feet of space), while a quarter consists of smaller warehouses, followed by cross-docking operations and refrigerated facilities. Over the next five years, respondents felt that bulk warehousing and cross-docking would become more prevalent.

   The reasons for this, besides the expected reasons of increases in throughput and storage capacity needs, were an increase in order complexity and a change in the outbound load profile. This is primarily driven by e-commerce growth and SKU proliferation.

2) **Market Pressures and Fulfillment Impact**

   Not surprisingly, "fulfillment responsiveness" is the capability whose importance has increased the most over the last five years. Years ago, you were lucky if an order was processed and shipped within the current week. Today, partially thanks to e-commerce (and lean supply chains), most consumer orders are processed and shipped within 24 hours (and many by the end of the current working day).

   "Fulfillment adaptability" (defined as the ability to handle a wide range of order profiles) has also risen in importance, even more than "fulfillment throughput", as the impact of omni-channel retail has increased overall order variability, making adaptability more important.

3) **Changing Fulfillment Methods**

While there are a variety of fulfillment methods to support such as traditional store replenishment, downstream DC replenishment, drop-shipping, and direct-to-consumer shipping (with store and DC replenishment being the most common), the survey respondents identified direct-to-consumer shipping and drop-shipping (shipping goods directly from the manufacturer) as the methods that would see the biggest growth.

This seems to indicate that e-commerce and omni-channel are not only affecting retailers, but also their manufacturing and wholesale partners. As retailers continue to see pressure on margins and, with omni-channel, are refocusing on the customer experience, many are passing parts of their inventory carrying costs and fulfillment processes onto their upstream partners through drop-shipping, which can also offer a way for retailers and manufacturers to increase revenues and improve customer service.

4) **Pick and Pack**

As has been stated previously, the balance among material handling units (pallet, case, piece) within a warehouse is changing concurrently with the adjustments in fulfillment channels. So, not surprisingly, the ARC survey found that respondents expect piece and case picking will increase while pallets decrease, as warehouses fulfill more e-commerce orders and upstream partners continue to offer greater SKU variability along with smaller volumes of the same SKU.

5) **Pain Points and the Need for Technology Investment**

Higher volumes of more variable, small multiline-item orders are raising fulfillment costs within the warehouse. While this requires lean, agile warehouse operations, the use of targeted technology can enable an efficient fulfillment process.

The areas most targeted by survey respondents for increased use of technology were shipping, goods retrieval/order picking, and put-away.

They also would want to be able to pick single- and multi-unit orders by zone within the same wave, as well as having flexible picking solutions that can be deployed at scale.

This and other ARC studies found that while e-commerce growth has led to an increase in parcel shipping, many practitioners also plan to invest in technology to support re-slotting and facility layout changes.

As far as software, the top priorities were labor management, as e-commerce fulfillment is labor-intensive, since the orders are small, often stored in different parts of the facility, and require additional steps such as packaging and labeling. Warehouse management systems (WMS) were also high on the software list.

Pick/put-to-light (along with conveyors/sortation) was a top automation hardware technology requiring investment, reflecting a desire to gain efficiencies in e-commerce fulfillment operations.

In summary, warehouse fulfillment is increasingly playing a greater role in commerce due to disintermediation (i.e. the removal of intermediaries in economics from a supply chain or bypassing the middleman) and a reduction in retail sales through stores. There is also a changing relationship between retailers and upstream partners, as retailers have pushed some direct-to-consumer responsibilities back onto their suppliers [Reiser, 2016].

DESIGNING DISTRIBUTION CENTERS FOR OMNI-CHANNEL FULFILLMENT

So how can you design omni-channel fulfillment operations to navigate the ever-changing concept as we are rapidly moving towards both "order from anywhere" *and* "fulfill from anywhere" models? For example, Best Buy has kiosks in hotels and airports where you can purchase various small tech products on the spot, and Target (and a number of other major retailers) is reportedly shipping from about 1,000 of its stores, which is a bit more than half of the facilities in the chain.

To do this of course requires you to transform the way your organization manages inventories and fulfills orders. Here are five tips when developing your omni-channel fulfillment operations strategy:

1. Look for similarities across channels – Look at potential synergies across product types, as well as identifying opportunities to pull inventories together across retail, e-commerce, wholesale, and other channels. Similarities may be found in a variety of areas including cycle time, packaging, inventory sharing, receiving/cross-dock,

put-away and storage, order profiles, picking methodology, value-added services, packing, shipping/carrier, and reverse logistics.

Some examples would include reduced safety stock from inventory sharing and leveraging similar picking methods across channels.

2. Find and select the best operating model – Develop an operating model that can exploit the similarities in order profiles and that defines order routing, order fulfillment locations, and other key elements of the omni-channel fulfillment process.

    For example, you may find that it makes sense to use static slotting for high pick productivity for fast-moving items and dynamic slotting for the rest of your slower-moving SKUs.

3. Choose technology to automate the process flow – Technology should to conform to your operating model and processes (not the other way around which is so often the case), and function across your organization's order management, ERP, e-commerce, mobile app, and other systems.

    This involves evaluating and finding the most financially justified technologies/processes and asking, "Will the improvements using a certain solution justify the investment?" This question can be asked in many fulfillment areas including receiving, picking (full and less than a case), replenishment, buffer/staging, packing, shipping/outbound, etc.

    For instance, to execute on the example in #2 above, some WMS can dynamically bring these items forward for slotting as needed to balance pick productivity with space utilization, which may be easy to justify in certain situations.

4. Optimize flow paths – Combine information from multiple databases for different types of customers using analytics into a unified view of the customer to gain visibility of the information you need to optimize flow paths and serve customers better.

    For example, you may find that a specific flow path for picking may only be applied to retail and wholesale orders, but for sortation and packing, e-commerce and only some wholesale orders can share a unit sorter. See Figure 11.1 for some examples.

    Also, there may be a need to re-purpose a fulfillment engine and shift some volume to an alternate flow path, if, for example, unexpected growth occurs in the primary flow path.

    This is a consideration in design as well, as most omni-channel fulfillment centers need a flexible ("flex") area to deal with the changes in mix across order profiles on any given day.

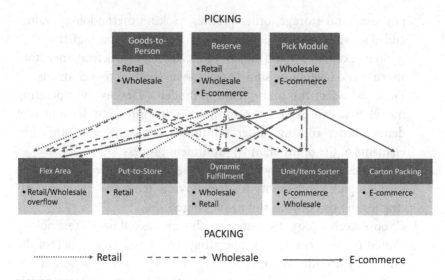

FIGURE 11.1
Common flows and connection points between picking and packing.

5. Implement function-specific technologies – Identify and implement function-specific technologies for the pick, pack, and ship process. For example, some picking options include paper, RF device, and by voice or by light. Sorters come in a variety of types (cross-belt, tilt tray, bomb bay, shoe, etc.), and goods-to-person technologies (i.e. a modern method of order fulfillment where product is moved directly to the operator, via carousel, AS/RS, etc., who can then pick what is needed to fulfill orders) vary as well.

   Technologies should support your operating model and flow paths, automating and integrating as much of the omni-channel flow as possible and delivering large customer service improvements to your customers [TotalRetail, 2013].

FULFILLMENT FROM STORE (FFS)

In Chapter 10 we discussed the fulfillment of omni-channel orders from stores a bit. Now is a good time to examine its impact a little more. While we keep hearing about all of the brick-and-mortar closures, the news of their death is slightly exaggerated as the saying goes. In many instances, it's more about changing their role to maximize value, as we know that people still like to leave their homes so that they can shop, compare, and pick up items that they are interested in purchasing.

As the omni-channel concept is all about offering a seamless customer experience across all channels, it is important to focus on three areas per the findings of VDC research (2018):

1. Cross-channel order fulfillment and distribution – Consolidate distribution channels to improve efficiency and respond to customer demands.
2. Customer engagement – Move away from "the product" to the "in-store experience".
3. Inventory visibility – Have a comprehensive, real-time view of all inventory (not just in the distribution center but also in transit for store replenishment, in retail stockrooms, and on the store floor) to help utilize inventory more efficiently.

The fulfillment from store (FFS) concept is based on treating the retail location's stock as part of the entire inventory that can fulfill any customer's purchase. Store associates can be equipped with mobile devices. If the retailer's omni-channel order management system determines that the inventory in a store location is the best choice to fulfill the order, the store associate pulls the product and ships it, or prepares for it to be picked up in the store.

To enable the FFS concept, inventory integration must be complete, real-time, and accurate and consists of these elements:

Stock receiving: Inventory accuracy starts at receiving; if it's not accurate when it enters the store stockroom, it's much harder to correct errors that pop up later.
Stock movement: Requires accurate and real-time tracking within the store, from stockroom to rack, to point of sale. This includes items pulled from store inventory and set aside for either FFS or for transfer to another retail location.
Stock counting: Use mobile-based tools so employees can "cycle count" inventory by department or store, to keep each store's inventory as accurate as possible.

Click-and-collect: Use tools to manage e-commerce orders for pickup at the store. BOPIS systems (one form of "click-and-collect") handle orders picked up from store inventory, manage order packing, labeling, parcel storage and retrieval, notify customers of order status, and complete the sales process when customers arrive.

Some retailers are purchasing packaged mobile tools and hardware to handle these FFS processes. However, many are working with third-party suppliers who can provide comprehensive solutions, including hardware, software, integration with existing inventory systems, and consulting [Felker, 2018].

RETAILERS SEEK TO TWEAK THE LAST MILE

As mentioned in Chapter 10, the growth of e-commerce and omni-channel retail is forcing brick-and-mortar retailers to become more creative about last-mile delivery, which not only has an impact on the supply chain network but perhaps even more on the fulfillment operations.

E-commerce has complicated the last mile of delivery at the consumer's home or business, making it much more challenging for retailers. Besides traditional home package last-mile delivery by companies like USPS, FedEx, and UPS, e-commerce businesses like Amazon have been exploring air and land drone delivery and lockers in pre-designated, mostly urban locations available for customer pickup. Earlier this year, the Washington Post reported on how Walmart is adding FedEx office locations, where customers can ship packages, drop off returns, and pick up deliveries, to 500 of its U.S. stores.

Traditional last-mile delivery involves many challenges including cost minimization, transparency, and efficiency. That, along with the growth of e-commerce, is forcing brick-and-mortar retailers to become more creative.

There is now an ongoing trend where large retailers such as Walmart and Best Buy use their brick-and-mortar stores as distribution centers. Basically, store employees pick items from the store shelves and backrooms to fulfill online orders and either drop them into waiting FedEx or UPS trucks or in some cases – currently being tested in a few Walmart stores in New Jersey and Arkansas, according to the Los Angeles Times – deliver packages themselves on their way home.

In the case of the Walmart employee delivery, they will use an app to specify how many packages they are willing to deliver and the maximum weight and sizes of the packages and will be paid for their efforts.

In any case, stores can stand to cut a significant amount of costs by having employees deliver from stores, as the "last-mile" costs for delivery are a significant part of fulfillment costs. Employee delivery is potentially even better than having a third party such as UPS or even Uber drivers do it (also being tested) as they would have to drive to the store, whereas the employee is already there. Furthermore, in the case of Walmart, two-thirds of the U.S. population live within five miles of a Walmart.

Some other benefits of retailers enabling last-mile delivery include switching online orders to locations with the most inventory of a selected item, thereby reducing the need for discounts, and fulfilling orders for items that are out of stock at e-commerce fulfillment centers (happens 2–4 percent of the time at Best Buy, for example).

This concept is even more important as Amazon continues to expand its network fulfillment centers closer to customers. By enabling store delivery, traditional retailers feel they can better compete with Amazon's fulfillment network of 100+ distribution centers by utilizing their hundreds or even thousands of brick-and-mortar locations as DCs.

If you are going to go down the road of ship-from-store fulfillment, a recent article in Parcel magazine offers some tips on picking and packing within the store, which, in addition to delivery, has a significant impact on costs and service:

Simplify the process – Establish standard operating procedures for picking and packing.

Maximize space – Determine what non-revenue-generating space is available and package to minimize space.

Deliver trust and excitement – Put some time and thought into packaging as it will impact customer satisfaction.

Reduce costs – Choose the right packaging as physical characteristics impact shipping costs.

Free up the phone lines – As you don't want damages and returns, select the right packaging (i.e. cushioning, wrapping, etc.) to protect the products.

Total cost over price – When deciding on packaging, consider the lowest cost to adequately protect your products during transit.

These are exciting but rapidly changing times for retail. Those who want to survive and thrive need to do their best to stay ahead of the curve, and one way that many are trying to do it is by focusing on the last mile of delivery [Myerson, 2018c].

Now that we've considered the impact of omni-channel retail on your fulfillment operations (i.e. the nodes in your supply chain network), it's important to consider the impact on transportation or the "links" in your network as well.

12

Impact of Omni-Channel Retail on Transportation Operations

There are many ways to get a product from a brick-and-mortar storefront, distribution center, or even a manufacturer to the customer's hands (whether that ultimate destination is at home, a store, or a locker for example), not to mention the expanding modes of transportation delivery available including private and public motor carriers, small package delivery vans, store employees, air and land drones, and the customer themselves of course. The challenge is to find the most effective and efficient transportation solution to keep customers happy without driving up the landed product costs. Selecting the right shipping method for the right customer situation is essential to omni-channel logistics.

These general shifts in consumer behavior point to a need for faster shipping to a wider range of destinations. But these movements don't exist in isolation. They are happening at the same time as the freight sector experiences a capacity and driver shortage, and manufacturers face mounting pressure to create more customized product lines and implement service-oriented shipping models.

In an attempt to accommodate the need for faster shipping, changing regulations, and infrastructure limitations, transportation and logistics providers have begun to research and offer alternative delivery solutions including click-to-collect locations (also known as buy online, pick up in-store (BOPIS)), drones, robots, local regional delivery services, Uber delivery, and more (Figure 12.1).

These changing demand patterns can also have a negative effect on transportation costs. So, when planning your omni-channel strategy, increased transportation cost is a big contributor to escalating fulfillment

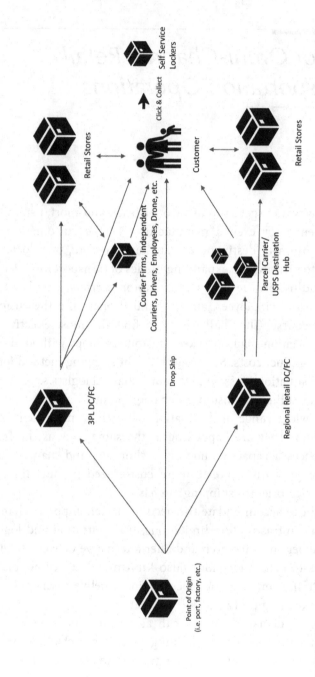

FIGURE 12.1
Last-mile delivery options.

costs for omni-channel operations. In a PwC survey (2016), 67 percent of CEOs said their fulfillment costs were increasing and that the costs to ship direct to customers (67 percent) and to ship to stores for customer pickup (59 percent) were the second and third biggest contributors to these rising costs (just behind the cost of returns at 71 percent).

Consumer demand for "buy anywhere, pick up anywhere, deliver anywhere" shopping experiences won't let transportation be an afterthought, as the Wall Street Journal has reported that fulfillment costs are on the rise across the retail industry. As revenues rise, fulfillment costs also go up, as retailers have seen a 300 percent increase in the cost-to-serve for omni-channel customers. It's been estimated that 18 cents out of every dollar generated online go to the costs of fulfillment. In the Retail Industry Leader Association's annual survey (as reported in Supply Chain Quarterly), controlling supply chain costs was identified as a top strategic priority for 2017 with omni-channel costs being a significant part of the picture. Just 50 percent of respondents recover some of the costs of omni-channel fulfillment, 40 percent don't recover any of the costs, and 10 percent aren't measuring it.

Today's best in class omni-channel leaders often have the ability to:

- Segment the supply chain based on customer profile data and manage these shipping and supply chain processes as a single connected entity to accelerate operations and eliminate inefficiencies.
- Maintain online visibility of fulfillment costs.
- Track actual costs as shipments/orders progress.
- Gain cost-to-serve modeling capabilities down to the product, customer, or location level.
- Optimize carrier sourcing to use the best possible shipping specialist for each product and delivery type, potentially implementing multi-modal capabilities to improve processes around omni-channel experiences.

Positioning the right inventory and assortments close to customer delivery points is critical for achieving customer satisfaction and profitability.

At the same time, it appears that, at least for now, CEOs are focusing more on growing revenues than on profitability, as the PwC survey (2016) of retailers found that the number one initiative (57 percent) was spending capital on creating new customer experiences, closely followed (56 percent) by using stores as fulfillment centers for faster deliveries of online purchases, and when asked to rank strategic growth enablers, reducing/reformatting physical store footprints to focus on expanding their e-commerce business was the top choice at 53 percent.

MANAGING LAST-MILE COSTS AND EFFICIENCY IS CRITICAL

Last-mile delivery is a critical part of an organization's transportation network, as it can make up 28 percent of a shipment's total cost. This is especially true with the emergence of e-commerce and omni-channel retail.

To be clear, last-mile delivery refers to the final step of the fulfillment process, from a distribution center, store, or other facility, such as a manufacturer when drop-shipping, to the end user where the actual "last mile" can range from a few blocks to up to 100 miles. Last-mile delivery has typically involved the use of parcel or small package carriers (but has expanded to store employees and even drones) to deliver products to consumers. As a result, the last mile can have a significant impact on both growth and profitability.

For example, Amazon's e-commerce business lost $7.2 billion from shipping in 2016, which was basically the difference between their shipping cost and what they charged for it (they made up for that loss through Amazon Web Services (AWS), with a 2016 corporate profit of $2.4 billion).

However, they are reducing their transportation expenses on a per-package and per-order basis every quarter of every year. In fact, by 2018 AWS and Amazon (e-commerce) North America had operating incomes (net sales, less operating expenses) of $7.3 billion each. It should be noted that it took $141.4 billion in sales for Amazon North America to accomplish this, while AWS only needed $25.65 billion.

At Amazon, items are typically warehoused within 90 miles of each customer so they lower shipping prices as they're moving items the shortest distance to the customer. Beyond that, they are now creating a network of "Amazon Logistics" partners, to expand their Delivery Service Partner (DSP) program, in which the company helps small business owners start their own companies to deliver Amazon packages and reduce last-mile costs even more from local facilities.

Another example can be found at Walmart which offers free two-day shipping for some $35+ orders with no membership fees (in addition to a free pickup in-store option for many items as well as store fulfillment and shipping which they are testing at various stores). For items priced below that, they charge $5.99 for shipping and handling (i.e. handling = fulfillment). Shipping costs alone are $2.50 minimum, rising to $3.50 to $5 depending on the shipping distance and the cube size, a fee that covers both fulfillment and shipping.

With free shipping, there's not necessarily a correlation between what's charged for shipping and the actual cost. The retailer makes the decision to offer it based on a business strategy, which might be merging the costs into the product price, increasing the sales dollars to qualify, or some other tactic.

For example, Alpha Industries, a military-inspired fashion retailer, uses a shipping pricing model which is promotionally based, offering a discount coupled with free shipping around certain holidays.

In any case, it is important that the retailer understands the true economics of their business to decide at what point free shipping pays off (including knowing the total landed cost of items), while making money as an entity and returning shareholder value.

As e-commerce includes residential deliveries as well as B2B deliveries, carriers are seeing a steady increase in last-mile delivery (for example, 40 percent of all FedEx's U.S. deliveries now go to residences). So, retailers and carriers need to work together when designing a last-mile strategy for omni-channel retail.

Some Ideas to Reduce Last-Mile Transportation Costs

As "free shipping" isn't really free, there are some ways retailers can reduce transportation costs:

> Offer a range of shipping options – For Alpha, that means offering cus-
> tomers several shipping options, including ground, two-day, and
> overnight shipping. And usually charging for it. However, they've
> negotiated competitive rates with UPS, and continue to negotiate
> new rates as the e-commerce business grows.

Drop off at access point – Shippers may charge less for recipients to pick up their packages at a central point (in essence, the customer becomes the "last-mile delivery"), like the retailer's store, as it's less expensive to deliver more packages to one location. That can have a positive impact on the retailer, who may get additional sales from the customer at pickup.

Limiting the travel distance – Some companies choose to use regional fulfillment centers or even stores to lower shipping costs and, as mentioned previously, some larger chains are experimenting with using their brick-and-mortar stores as fulfillment centers, vs. warehouses, so the packages travel shorter distances (for example, it is estimated that 90 percent of all Americans live within 15 miles of a Walmart).

Change the box size – Many small to medium-size retailers buy cardboard boxes in small quantities, so they tend buy the size in the middle to save on costs, which may be bigger than they need, wasting valuable cubic space when it comes to transportation costs. They can work with carriers to design and buy more appropriately sized packaging, to decrease transportation costs [Kaplan, 2017].

HOW OMNI-CHANNEL FULFILLMENT IS AFFECTING TRANSPORTATION SOURCING AND EXECUTION

Traditional carrier transportation models are not designed to handle the challenges of omni-channel service, especially in the area of "ship from store" and "pickup at store" fulfillment models which require multi-stop planning for last-mile deliveries and advanced scheduling capabilities, along with end-to-end visibility of order location and status for the customer.

As a distinct subset of omni-channel commerce, last-mile deliveries pose a different set of challenges that must be understood and met. These include more sophisticated planning for multi-stop routing, tight delivery windows, and more frequent non-dock deliveries to residences and businesses.

Internally, there is often not a clear picture of who owns transportation in this omni-channel environment. In some cases, the person who owns the parcel side and the last mile reports to the e-commerce team, not the transportation team that is responsible for the rest of the company's transportation operations.

Omni-channel fulfillment also affects transportation sourcing and execution in that you need to understand that, as you're talking about a different model, you can't just use your baseline data set and requirements in the bidding process and expect to be successful.

You have to understand that you're talking about a different model with "ship to store" and "ship from store" as they are different concepts from what many companies have dealt with before when developing a transportation sourcing strategy.

For example, in the case of a large brick-and-mortar store chain with 4,000 stores, moving to omni-channel required them to use a combination of static and dynamic routes that used less-than-truckload or multi-stop-truckload weekly shipments to stores coupled with parcel deliveries in between to replenish fast-selling critical products driven by point-of-sale data.

However, instead of using traditional metrics such as cost per hundred weight or cost per pound to determine if they should use a parcel network to deliver 25 cartons to a store, they instead looked at the sell-through rate and the gross margin that they're making by getting products back in stock faster. By doing that, they found that the amount of gross margin they made far outweighed the fact that they were going to spend more in transportation. In the end, the additional gross margin surpassed the transportation cost by ten to one.

In order to create an omni-channel transportation strategy, you must use a combination of traditional approaches plus strategies that also integrate omni-channel [Gonzalez, 2015].

WHERE IS LAST-MILE DELIVERY HEADED?

Today, retailers need to have great distribution, an online presence, and the ability to perform same-day delivery. In the United States, the delivery network is fragmented and often somewhat disorganized, so direct-to-consumer deliveries, same-day delivery of automotive parts, legal documents, and pharmaceutical and medical products as well as other goods had been handled by messenger and courier services. Now, with the tremendous increase in the need for direct-to-consumer deliveries from online stores, distribution patterns and delivery networks have evolved in multiple directions. From Amazon and Walmart to Uber drivers, last-mile delivery seems to have changed forever.

Not too long ago, a trend towards independent transportation and logistics providers started. Couriers with fleets of employees began to examine new ways to provide last-mile delivery service in more cost-effective ways.

In addition, retailers like Walmart and Target have also looked to supplement this by using employees to deliver packages ordered online from brick-and-mortar locations.

Amazon with its "Flex" program uses on-demand contract drivers to help with this especially labor-intensive and expensive hand-delivery, and also has started Amazon Delivery Service Partner (ADSP), seeking hundreds of entrepreneurs across the country to launch and operate their own Amazon package delivery business.

Below are some examples of how the supply chain industry is trying to solve the last-mile delivery challenge:

- Hyperlocal delivery services. Uber is a pioneer in this field.
- Retailers (and manufacturers) drop-shipping goods to consumers.
- Acquiring logistics providers such as the Target purchase of Shipt and Grand Junction.
- Acquisition of e-commerce companies by retailers such as the Walmart acquisition of Jet and Bonobos.

Speed of delivery is also a major challenge due to numerous factors, including traffic congestion, lack of transportation and logistics providers, and other challenges, with younger consumers having the highest desire for immediate delivery (which can also increase their loyalty to a retail brand). However, cost is still an issue as Amazon Prime has gotten many used to fast (within two days), free delivery.

It's gotten complicated with consumers regularly leaving instructions to deliver parcels to neighbors, put them out of sight, or customize the final-mile delivery in other ways.

Technology and the Last Mile

Innovation in technology has provided a glimmer of hope, with some of the latest trends below helping last-mile logistics providers to meet consumer demands:

1. Crowdsourced mobile apps for last mile delivery – Local non-professional delivery service providers transport packages to customers' doors, often on the same day, showing a lot of potential in speeding up deliveries in urban areas, as the high density of deliveries can be matched with potential couriers within the given area.

   Current crowdsourced last-mile delivery options include Postmates, Instacart, Deliv, and Hitch.

2. Cargo drones – Amazon, Google, Uber, and Airbus currently have R&D programs in this mode of delivery using plane-sized autonomous air delivery vehicles. In fact, cargo drones are used today in areas with challenging environments such as Africa and Canada to primarily transport medication to remote areas.

   Cargo drones may be important in the future of e-commerce fulfillment and last-mile delivery as, in urban areas, more parcels result in more vehicles, traffic congestion, and emissions and may even replace some delivery trucks and vans someday. However, there is quite a resistance currently to drones flying overhead in residential areas which would have to change for their success in urban areas.

3. Autonomous vehicles and delivery robots – Land drones or unmanned ground vehicles (UGVs), that operate while in contact with the ground and without an onboard human presence, may have a better chance for success as a delivery alternative in urban areas, at least in the shorter term. So, it's no surprise that from pizza and restaurant food to e-commerce parcels, autonomous guided vehicles (AGVs) are projected to gain momentum in the coming years.

   AGVs with parcel lockers have the potential to replace existing forms of regular parcel delivery, with up to a 40 percent reduction in delivery costs.

   It seems very "Jetsons-like" that the world would use drones and robots to deliver packages, but because of the boom in online shopping, the supply chain industry is turning to autonomous vehicles, crowdsourced delivery apps, and independent delivery drivers and other innovations for parcel delivery. Consumers expect fast, cost-effective delivery options, and last-mile technology may be at least part of the solution [Datex Corp, 2019].

   As the impact of omni-channel retail on the supply chain is substantial, many organizations are struggling with whether to cope with it on their own or with the help of partners, which is the topic of our next chapter.

13

The "Make or Buy" Decision: E-Commerce Fulfillment, Transportation, Technology, Customization, and Reverse Logistics

As retailers shift to omni-channel and their supply chains evolve along with it, they have to make the determination of whether to perform all or parts of the process internally, externally (i.e. outsourced), or through some blend (or "hybrid") of both.

The areas with the greatest impact involved in this "make or buy" decision are the e-commerce business itself (i.e. the e-commerce website and other technologies), order fulfillment, transportation, customization, and reverse logistics.

If you're a larger company, it may be worth considering creating all of the aforementioned processes and technologies in-house, with a bigger investment up front. This would include hiring IT staff to build entirely new business process workflows and supporting systems, investing in software and hardware. Your distribution facility and processes, inventory, 3PL relationships, shipping, carriers, and other services related to moving around products will need to be retooled. If you are going this route, it would be a good idea to get assistance from an experienced system integrator with a lot of experience in these types of projects.

On the other hand, you can gain many of the benefits of omni-channel retail by outsourcing the e-commerce side of your business, marketing, EDI, fulfillment, and other processes. This may be a better (starting) option for small to medium-sized enterprises (SMEs), because the costs to get started with omni-channel retail in this fashion tend to be lower than doing it in-house. However, there will still be costs associated with whatever services you outsource such as setup, training, vendor management, etc.

A hybrid system is also worth considering, with some services and processes brought in-house and others outsourced. This allows a retailer to migrate key processes to the Web over time but still get started quickly without major disruptions. This strategy isn't only for small retailers though, as retailers of all sizes leverage hybrid systems to create seamless omni-channel experiences, internalize specific functions that are core competencies and/or critical success factors in their industry, and outsource areas with more proven external solutions or those needing to scale more quickly, such as EDI and logistics.

The supply chain and logistics function is always a prime candidate for outsourcing. Strategically speaking, most successful companies stay with their core competencies and let outside entities help with the rest.

This can range from the outsourcing of functional areas such as materials, transportation, warehouse services, and manufacturing to the almost entire outsourcing of an organization, known as a "virtual company".

There are four major ways to get things done in business. They are:

1. Internal – Processes that are core competencies are usually the best way to perform an activity.
2. "Arm's-length" transactions – Most business transactions are of this type. These are short-term arrangements that meet a particular business need but don't lead to long-term strategic advantages.
3. Strategic alliances – Longer term multifaceted partnerships between two companies that are goal-oriented. There are both risks and rewards to an alliance, which are shared, but alliances can lead to long-term strategic benefits for both partners. Strategic alliances in the supply chain include third-party (3PL) and fourth-party (4PL) logistics services.
4. Acquisition – Gives the acquiring firm full control over the way the particular business function is performed. Can be difficult and expensive (e.g. changing culture, acquisition costs, etc.).

THE "MAKE OR BUY" DECISION

One of the first decisions to consider in regard to supply chain management processes, at least strategically, is the question of "make or buy", which is the choice between internal production and external sources.

A simple break-even analysis can be used to quickly determine the cost implications of a make or buy decision in the following example...

If a firm can purchase equipment for in-house use for $500,000 and produce requested parts for $20 each (*assume there is no excess capacity on their current equipment*) or they can have a supplier produce and ship the parts for $30 each, what would be the correct decision ... make (assume with new equipment) or buy (i.e. outsource production)?

To arrive at the correct decision, a simple break-even point could easily be calculated as follows:

$$\$500,000 + \$20Q = \$30Q$$
$$\$500,000 = \$30Q - \$20Q$$
$$\$500,000 = \$10Q$$
$$50,000 = Q$$

As the break-even point is 50,000 units, the answer is that it would be better for the firm to buy the part from a supplier if demand is less than 50,000 units and purchase the necessary equipment to make the part if demand is greater than 50,000 units.

OUTSOURCING AS A STRATEGY

Outsourcing is the contracting out of business processes, activities, or resources to a third party, where an organization transfers some internal activities and resources of a firm to outside vendors. It is really an extension of the sub-contracting and contract manufacturing of product, which have both existed for a very long time. Outsourcing includes both foreign and domestic contracting and can include "offshoring" or relocating a business function to another country.

Many companies choose to outsource activities, resources, and entire business processes for a variety of reasons that include not being viewed as a core competency, high taxes, high energy costs, excessive government regulation, and high production or labor costs.

Most firms outsource some functions in which they don't feel that they have a competency, such as the fulfillment of orders as in the printing industry, using for-hire motor carriers for delivery to customers, or reverse logistics, which is common in many industries.

In the 1990s, to reduce costs, companies began to outsource a variety of services such as accounting, human resources, technology, internal mail distribution, security, and facility maintenance.

From a supply chain standpoint, there are a variety of functions that may be candidates for outsourcing such as warehousing, transportation, freight audit and payment, procurement, and customer service/call centers.

In today's global economy, organizations look for long-term, strategic partnerships for functions and services, some that might even be considered "core competencies", to gain a strategic advantage. The rapid increase in outsourcing can at least partially be attributed to increased technological expertise, more reliable and less costly transportation service, and advancements in telecommunications and computer systems.

Reasons to Outsource

Some reasons to outsource include:

- Lower operational and labor costs – These are usually the primary reasons why companies choose to outsource. When properly executed it has a defining impact on a company's revenue and can deliver large savings.
- Company focus – So that a company can continue to focus on core business processes and competencies while delegating less important, time-consuming processes to external partners.
- Knowledge – It can enable companies to leverage a global knowledge base and have access to world-class capabilities.
- Freeing up internal resources – They can be put to more effective use for other purposes.
- Access to resources not available internally – Companies may have internal resource constraints.
- Specialists for hard-to-manage areas – By delegating responsibilities to external agencies, companies can hand off functions that are difficult to manage and control while still realizing their benefits.

- Risk mitigation – Outsourcing and especially offshoring help companies to mitigate risk.
- Re-engineering – Can enable companies to realize the benefits of a re-engineering process.
- New markets – Some companies may outsource to help them expand and gain access to new market areas, by moving the point of production or service delivery closer to their end users.

Steps in the Outsourcing Process

Outsourcing, which in many ways is similar to any sourcing (of goods or services) initiative, must follow a distinct process in order to be successful. A good example of one methodology is encompassed in the following steps:

Step 1: Plan initiatives – Establish cross-functional teams to assess the risks and resources. The team sets objectives, deliverables, and time-tables and is responsible for achieving critical management "buy-in".

This step should also include sharing the information with employees. If not, employees may assume the worst, causing a lowering of morale.

Step 2: Explore strategic implications – This is the step in which using outsourcing as a strategic tool examines current and future organizational structures and considers current and future core competencies. It is a long-term view to see if the solution is a good fit.

Step 3: Analyze cost and performance – The organization must next make sure that all costs needed to support the activity, direct and indirect, are considered. Current performance must also be measured and analyzed to establish a baseline against which to measure improvement.

Step 4: Select providers – Finding potential providers can be done in a variety of ways, including the use of references from business associates, directories, advertisements, requests for information (RFIs), etc.

Once you have narrowed the list of potential outsource partners, you'll need to develop and send out requests for proposals (RFPs) or requests for quotes (RFQs). The RFPs should at least include what is required of the outsourcer in the way of both services and information. Once returned, RFPs should be evaluated in terms of both qualifications and cost.

Step 5: Negotiate terms – You should next map out with the provider the services to be provided and pricing (including how changes in scope or volume will be handled), as well as performance standards, management issues, and transition and termination provisions. A clear, well-documented understanding during this process can contribute greatly to the success of the relationship. The organization also needs to consider worst-case scenarios, which outline a plan of action should the outsourcing relationship fail.

Step 6: Transition resources – One of the biggest challenges to the staff of the organization is managing the impact of the potential change and the actual transition. Open communication from the start is critical.

Human resource issues should be carefully addressed, and with sensitivity. Any staff that are about to be terminated because their jobs have been outsourced should be treated with sensitivity and respect. This will have an impact on how the remaining employees, who were not outsourced, contribute in the future. So, providing terminated employees such benefits as outplacement services is a good idea when possible.

Step 7: Manage the relationship – Outsourcing requires a different set of skills, as, besides scheduled meetings and reports, unforeseen things may come up. So, in addition to monitoring performance and evaluating results, a relationship of trust that enables problem solving is critical with your outsourcing partner [Greaver, 1999].

SUPPLY CHAIN AND LOGISTICS OUTSOURCING PARTNERS

Traditional Service Providers

In the supply chain and logistics function, the two traditional service providers are in the areas of transportation and warehousing.

The for-hire transportation industry has thousands of carriers who specialize in product movement between geographic locations and provide an assortment of services in various modes of transportation with related technology.

For-hire transportation companies offer specialization, efficiency, and scale economies to their customers. The choice for users of these services is to invest in and operate the vehicles themselves or use for-hire services at a negotiated (or standard) rate.

Public warehouses also offer storage and value-added services on a contracted basis, with the customer having similar choices as were mentioned for transportation (i.e. invest capital or "pay as you go").

The main benefits of using public vs. private warehousing is that there is no capital investment required for the building and equipment (and no employees to hire and manage) and the potential to consolidate small shipments with products of other firms that use the same public warehouse for combined delivery at a lower transportation rate. The warehouse charges are both time (i.e. storage) and/or transaction (i.e. handling and specialized services) based, as stated in the contract.

Third-Party Logistics Provider (3PL)

A third-party logistics provider (3PL) is an external supplier that performs all or part of its customers' outsourced logistics functions and is usually asset-based (although not always, as in the case of a financial services, freight forwarding or information systems-based firm).

Most typically, 3PLs specialize in integrated operation, warehousing, and transportation services based upon their customers' needs, which may vary based upon market conditions and delivery service requirements for their products and materials.

In the 1970s and 1980s, mostly operational, repetitive, transactional operations were outsourced in the logistics function of an organization that required the use of the service provider's transportation management system (TMS) and warehouse management system (WMS) (Figure 13.1).

By 2018, the global 3PL industry had grown to an estimated $728 billion in size ($189 billion in the U.S.) and in addition to basic warehouse and transportation services, many 3PLs now offer value-added services related to the production or procurement of goods such as order fulfillment, labeling, packaging, assembly, kitting, reverse logistics, information technology services, customs brokering, cross-docking, and forwarding.

As a result of its far-reaching impact, the relationship between an organization and a 3PL vendor is a strategic, long-term, multi-functional partnership.

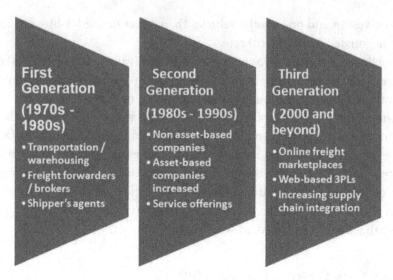

FIGURE 13.1
Evolution of third-party logistics service providers.

Advantages and Disadvantages of a 3PL

Advantages

There are many advantages to using 3PL service providers. They include:

Focus on core strengths – Allows a company to focus on its core competencies and leave logistics to the experts.

Provides technological flexibility – Technology advances are adopted by better 3PL providers in a quicker, more cost-effective way than doing it yourself. 3PLs may already have the capability to meet the needs of a firm's potential customers.

Flexibility – The use of a 3PL offers companies flexibility in geographic locations, service offerings, resources, and workforce size.

Cost savings – 3PLs offer the economic principle of specialization by building up logistical infrastructures, methodologies, and computer-based algorithms to maximize shipping efficiency to cut a client's logistics costs.

Capabilities – Smaller companies have to make large investments to expand their logistic capabilities. It may be more cost-effective and quicker to add capabilities through a third-party logistics provider.

Disadvantages

Disadvantages of using 3PLs include:

Loss of control in outsourcing a particular function – As most 3PLs are on the outbound side, they heavily interact with an organization's customers. Knowing that, many third-party logistics firms work very hard to address these concerns by doing things such as painting client company logos on the sides of trucks, dressing 3PL employees in the uniforms of the hiring company, and providing extensive reporting on each customer interaction.

Pricing models – By handing logistics over to a 3PL service, you may be missing out on the possibility that an in-house logistics department could come up with a cheaper and more efficient solution.

Dependency – If a 3PL is not working out as expected, switching a company's logistical support can cost the company a great deal in unanticipated costs resulting from the changes in pricing or unsatisfactory service reliability from the 3PL service.

Logistics is one of the core competencies of a firm – In this case, it makes no sense to outsource these activities to a supplier who may not be as capable as the firm's in-house expertise.

3PL: Example

Ryder is one of the largest and most recognizable 3PL brand names. They are a lead logistics provider for most General Motors plants and service Chrysler/Fiat, Toyota, and Honda plus a multitude of tier-one suppliers. Among their services, they run inbound supply chain management, sequencing centers, just-in-time, and dedicated contract carriage operations for clients.

Some results that Ryder has had with clients include:

Apria Healthcare – In 2012, Apria contracted with Ryder Supply Chain Services (SCS) to provide dedicated contract carriage (DCC) dry-van truckload transportation services for products moving from its seven DCs and cross-dock to its branch operations. As part of the operation, Ryder SCS also manages unattended deliveries, hazardous materials, product segregation, and vendor returns.

The following actions were taken:

- The majority of inbound supplier shipments consolidated onto full truckloads (over 75 percent of shipments now move at truckload rates).
- Supplier shipment frequency reduced to one to two times per week to each Apria DC.
- Expedited freight greatly reduced, and the standard shipment method is now truckload and less-than-truckload.
- The network has been optimized by filling Ryder's dedicated operation's backhaul lanes with inbound shipments from suppliers to Apria DCs.

Carrier Corporation (Mexico) – Ryder supports three Carrier air conditioner-related operations in and around Monterrey.

At the Carrier residential air conditioner factory in Monterrey, Ryder has 110 employees integrated with 1,100 Carrier employees. Ryder's personnel handle receiving, manufacturing (JIT/Kanban) support, and shipping. Ryder does all phases of the materials management for Carrier including sequencing, kitting, picking, and packing. Ryder also handles a large portion of inbound with dedicated and managed transportation for the facility [www.3plogistics.com, 2007, 2013].

Fourth-Party Logistics Service Provider (4PL)

A 4PL is an integrator that assembles not only the resources (including possibly 3PLs), but also the planning capabilities and technology of its own organization and other organizations to design, build, and run comprehensive supply chain solutions for clients.

This is as opposed to a 3PL service provider that typically targets a single function. A 4PL targets management of the entire process. In some ways a 4PL can be thought of as a general contractor that manages other 3PLs, transportation companies, forwarders, custom house agents, etc., and therefore takes responsibility for a complete process for the customer (Figure 13.2).

The key difference between 4PL and other approaches to supply chain outsourcing is a unique ability to deliver value to client organizations across the entire supply chain.

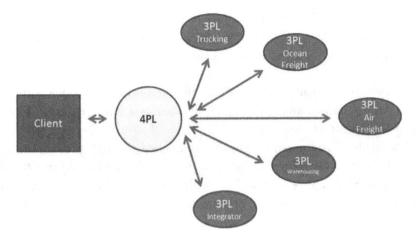

FIGURE 13.2
Fourth-party logistics service provider.

4PL service providers are able to combine multiple clients spend to take advantage of high-volume discounts which in turn enable them to provide affordable services to businesses of all sizes ranging from small e-commerce start-ups to multinational manufacturers.

4PLs come in many varieties. For example, UPS now offers 4PL service that includes global supply chain design and planning, logistics and distribution, customs brokerage, and international trade services, as well as freight services via ocean, air, and ground.

This is opposed to a 3PL service provider who usually focuses on one or two areas of expertise, such as warehousing, distribution, or freight forwarding, often resulting in multiple 3PLs being used to complete the supply chain.

4PL: The Players

The players involved in creating a 4PL organization are:

1) The client who provides start-up equity, some assets, working capital, operational expertise, and staff, and of course procures logistics services from a 4PL organization.
2) 3PL service providers (primarily for transportation services and distribution facilities).

3) The 4PL partner who may provide a range of resources including logistics strategy, reengineering skill, benchmarks, IT development, customer service and supplier management, and logistics consulting.

The typical 4PL organization is hybrid, in that it is formed from a number of different entities and typically established as a joint venture (JV) or long-term contract.

The goals of partners and clients are aligned through profit-sharing, and the hybrid 4PL organization is responsible for the management and operation of the entire supply chain with a continual flow of information between partners and the 4PL organization.

4PL: Components Required for Success

The components required for a successful 4PL strategy are:

1. Leadership – Must be a bit of a supply chain visionary and deal maker with multiple customer relationships. This component acts as the project manager as well as a service, systems, and information integrator.
2. Management – Experienced in logistics operations, optimization, and continuous improvement to run day-to-day operations and make important decisions. This component must also manage multiple 3PLs.
3. Information technology (IT) support – The "brains" of the operation with full integration and support of all systems in the supply chain.
4. Assets – Transportation and warehouse assets as well as outsourced contract manufacturing and co-packing and procurement services.

4PL: Example

Menlo Worldwide Logistics, now a subsidiary of XPO Logistics (www.xpo.com), is a leader in 4PL that specializes in the integration of all functions across the supply chain, from the sourcing of raw materials, through product manufacturing to the distribution of finished goods.

Menlo acts as a neutral single point of control for your supply chain by managing the procurement, optimization, information analytics, and operations of your supply chain network. They help their clients to create flexible supply chain solution that support their corporate strategy while increasing supply chain savings and service improvements. They act as a change agent to ensure the success of a client's supply chain transformation. They provide:

- Deployment of lean tools and methodologies.
- Self-funding initiatives.
- Delivery of flexible supply chains built to withstand business change and improve velocity.
- Delivery of best-of-breed and customer-specific business solutions.

To get an idea of what kind of success companies can have implementing a 4PL strategy, below are some results from some Menlo clients [www.con-way.com, 2014]:

Automotive customer – Managed more than 12,000 locations, $4 billion logistics spend with $648 million in savings. Utilized business case methodology to identify and measure savings.
High-tech customer – Over $30 million in savings throughout engagement, $9 million cost reduction through network rationalization and optimization in year one and integration of regional operations into enterprise-wide network.
Heavy equipment customer – Support $400 million global logistics network, on track to achieve a 25 percent reduction in supply chain spend. Cross business unit solutions including:
- Global transportation networks
- Regional infrastructure requirements
- New landed cost modeling

DIRECT-TO-CONSUMER (D2C) BRANDS

A variation on outsourcing (and the e-commerce model) used by many entrepreneurial and disruptive e-commerce businesses is direct-to-consumer (D2C), where companies manufacture and ship (both functions are often outsourced) their products directly to buyers without relying on traditional stores or other middlemen. This allows them to sell their products at lower costs than traditional consumer brands, and to maintain end-to-end control over the manufacturing and distribution and marketing of products.

D2C brands can experiment with distribution models, from shipping directly to consumers, to partnerships with physical retailers, to opening pop-up shops. They don't need to rely on traditional retail stores for exposure, but many use Amazon for (partial) distribution of their products or to create niches away from Amazon's marketplace.

Some examples of startups using this method are Casper, which is taking on the mattress industry; Dollar Shave Club and Harry's are taking on the razor industry; and The Honest Company is upending the cleaning and baby products segment [CB Insights, 2019].

D2C for Manufacturers

Manufacturers have historically leveraged a network of distributors and resellers as the simplest way to get their products to the end users.

Third-party distributor groups have provided logistical support and warehousing and sales support, to allow manufacturers to focus on other matters like product design, process development, and quality control.

However, the emergence of omni-channel, as well as COVID-19, has accelerated the shift to direct-to-consumer sales. In fact, the D2C strategy is becoming a popular way for manufacturers and consumer packaged goods (CPG) brands to enter the market directly. Examples include luggage manufacturer Away and office supplies manufacturer Quill who have already taken the leap with D2C marketing and D2C selling campaigns.

While many manufacturers have limited their activities in omni-channel by occasionally drop-shipping on behalf of e-commerce customers, many are now putting serious effort toward growing awareness of their brands and creating a digital presence to compete with the experiences that consumers have with Amazon and other online retailers.

However, going D2C means the manufacturer takes responsibility for all things retail-related within the business in addition to their original manufacturing and fulfillment responsibilities.

While this added responsibility entails risks, the drivers for it can be great, as today's consumers expect to be able to go directly to the source when researching a variety of products or brands, or when making a purchase from a specific brand, not to mention that many consumers are going directly to the source, which means they aren't doing business with many traditional retailers at all.

OUTSOURCING CANDIDATES

While potentially any business process or activity can be a candidate for outsourcing (or pretty much all processes in the case of a "virtual company"), the main areas to be considered when it comes to omni-channel are e-commerce order fulfillment, transportation, technology, and reverse logistics.

While it is possible (and somewhat common) to outsource the entire e-commerce portion of your business with a 3PL for example, it can be challenging to totally integrate it for a true omni-channel customer experience. That being the case, we will look at some of the major processes or activities mentioned separately (and in some cases, there is overlap), while keeping in mind that 3PLs tend to offer more of a "one-stop shopping" type of choice for this as opposed to picking and choosing individual processes to outsource with various partners.

Order Fulfillment

An order fulfillment provider essentially stores goods (i.e. your products) for your clients. Once they receive an order, the fulfillment provider will pick, pack, and prepare and schedule the product for shipment from package delivery carriers.

Outsourcing order fulfillment processes to a third-party logistics (3PL) company means they handle services on your behalf using their infrastructure, workforce, and technology such as:

Warehousing – Storing and managing your inventory in the 3PL's facilities.

Picking – Following a pick list and retrieving the item(s) from their spot in the 3PLs warehouse as soon as an order is placed on your website.

Packing – Packaging all items in the order using the appropriate box or poly mailer and packing materials, then adding the shipping label to the package.

Shipping – Scheduling shipping carriers to pick up packages from the 3PL's facility to be sent to your customers along with electronic order tracking information.

Returns processing – Facilitating the returns process and getting your unused merchandise back into your available inventory.

The company you outsource fulfillment to should become a true partner for your business, not just a transactional vendor.

Benefits to Outsourcing Fulfillment Services

There are a number of benefits to outsourcing order fulfillment services, such as lower shipping rates, reduced operating costs, and a broader reach to help you grow into new markets. For example:

You will no longer have to store inventory yourself, and the service provider can efficiently track your inventory levels.

You don't have to deal with packing boxes, shipping carriers, running a warehouse, and other fulfillment tasks any longer, and you can grow the business by focusing on the most important tasks to build sales and serve your customer community.

You can leverage the 3PL's volume and fulfillment expertise as you grow as they know best practices, can handle peak season, scale their workforce, manage returns, etc.

If you fulfill orders in-house, you may be limited to shipping orders from one location, which can be more expensive and result in longer transit times for some customers.

You get the best technology and analytics to help your business grow.

Many fulfillment providers offer seamless integration to connect your entire supply chain to your sales channels, by:

- Offering expedited shipping options.
- Routing orders to the fulfillment center that is closest to the customer.
- Providing real-time tracking for orders.
- Making data-driven decisions using analytical reports to reduce shipping costs and transit times.
- Forecasting demand and inventory replenishment needs.

However, outsourcing fulfillment isn't for everyone and should be a strategic decision. You may want to keep it in-house for reasons such as a desire to maintain control of all steps in the fulfillment process, to provide some customization or other value-added services (which can also be outsourced if you so choose), or if sales volume is still low enough to handle it yourself for example.

The Process to Outsource Fulfillment Services

When considering outsourcing your fulfillment services, you should first determine your needs. This should include your growth plans, features you might need such as kitting or refrigeration, timeline, and branding needs related to packaging for example.

Next you need to evaluate qualified fulfillment providers as they directly impact your customers. When evaluating the providers, you should consider:

- Fulfillment costs – Make sure you understand all potential costs based upon your needs, as providers have to charge for all services to remain profitable.
- Location(s) – Do a thorough network analysis based upon customer locations, projected demands, transportation costs, and lead times to pick providers in optimal locations.
- Space – Will there be enough space not only for current needs but also future growth?
- Services – Can they provide adequate value-added services such as kitting, returns processing, etc., that you may need?
- Technology – Evaluate whether the provider has adequate access to technology and if your current online store(s) and the other systems in your e-commerce operations are compatible with their fulfillment solution. This includes reporting and other tools they offer to assist with everything from inventory forecasting to inventory distribution optimization.
- Support – Determine the support you will need to receive and if they can provide it, ranging from phone calls to dedicated on-site account management.

Outsourcing Technology

Technology is critical to an effective omni-channel operation with "intelligent sharing" of inventory across channels being a "best practice" today. This requires high-tech inventory and warehouse management systems for visibility and integration.

Many retailers and e-commerce companies invest in systems such as WMS packages; others find that the cost of these systems is more than they can afford. To be competitive and cost-effective, many choose to partner with third-party providers. Outsourcing gives companies a chance to leverage cutting-edge systems, automation, and expertise without a significant up-front investment.

It is important to select a provider with flexibility and agility as omni-channel orders can vary greatly including a combination of pallets, cases, and pieces. Fulfillment automation solutions can include pick-to-light technology, voice picking, RF scanners, etc., to help improve order turnaround and delivery times, keeping in mind that the processes may need to be customized for better efficiency.

Outsourcing of Customization Services

Many omni-channel supply chain solutions need to be customized to support a company's strategic goals.

Customized solutions need to be developed collaboratively with a multi-functional team made up of stakeholders from the company and the solution provider, while taking into account product characteristics, order profiles, business fluctuations, and customer expectations.

Postponement strategies can be a creative way to process orders faster, improve cycle times, and be responsive to customer demands as positioning value-added services like packaging and fulfillment as close to the customer as possible helps to satisfy their needs quickly and cost-effectively without a major overhead investment. It also helps to partially compensate for volatile forecasts, reduce inventory carrying and transportation costs, and increase time to market.

Outsourcing customized value-added services to a third-party provider can offer more scalability in terms of space and labor as well as access to state-of-the-art technology and equipment without the need to tie up capital.

📁 **CASE STUDY #1: OMNI-CHANNEL PARTNERSHIP**

A major footwear retailer that sells more than 17 million pairs annually partnered with Saddle Creek, a 3PL, to ensure integrated fulfillment across all sales channels.

Saddle Creek now fulfills the majority of the major footwear retailer's orders. In addition to store replenishment, they also manage the entire e-commerce channel and new store-set programs and all specialty store-support functions such as returns and seasonal resets for the entire nationwide footprint. Saddle Creek also implemented a highly configurable, cost-effective warehouse management solution in just six weeks. Furthermore, they delivered an RF solution which includes mobile wearable RF technology, gives users hands-free capability to handle the single-shoe units that are being processed to the stores and directly to the end customer through the retailer's e-commerce portal.

As Saddle Creek has full data integration with the retailer's multiple business units, there is a continuous flow of data to and from their host system to the Saddle Creek WMS.

The partnership has resulted in significant gains in customer service and order cycle times. Saddle Creek is also now deeply involved in their strategic planning and continuous improvement programs [Saddle Creek Logistics Services, 2016].

Transportation Services Outsourcing

Companies that need to handle large amounts of goods need warehouse space, but then the question becomes "how to transport everything in and out of that facility".

Some may buy a fleet of trucks, hire a staff of drivers, and add some coordinators to keep everything on track, which can be very expensive and complicated.

Most companies consider outsourced transportation services to handle their logistics needs, keeping in mind that some companies may only want to consider a transportation specialist; many others find it's better to choose a third-party logistics provider that also offers receiving and storage, order fulfillment, and transportation solutions to manage every step of the supply chain process.

Transportation services connected to warehouses handle a variety of pickup and delivery needs, such as shuttling materials between the factory and the warehouse, handling dock-to-dock deliveries between ports, rail yards, and airports, taking care of express and other special-delivery needs, and pick-and-pack distribution from the warehouse.

Outsourced warehousing and transportation are especially beneficial to e-commerce companies, as they need the ability to move hundreds or thousands of packages every day. By outsourcing, the owners of these businesses save themselves from making substantial investments in infrastructure, purchases, and staffing.

Reverse Logistics Services Outsourcing

While many retailers have significantly improved their forward logistics strategies with fast fulfillment and free shipping, with e-commerce, which means buying goods sight unseen, comes higher return rates, as high as30 percent for online sales.

The reverse supply chain has not been given the attention that it perhaps has deserved, with retailers using piecemeal solutions such as local liquidation vendors to handle returns.

For omni-channel retailers, deciding on using in-store vs. consolidated returns operations is an important question. The benefit of in-store is that stores can disposition and potentially resell some portion of the returns immediately. This of course also takes focus away from forward sales and operations.

Omni-channel retailers can generally find that handling some dispositions in-store is very efficient, for example returning qualified stock back to shelves and liquidating low retail price inventory at the physical store, while consolidating and sending the remaining inventory to centralized facilities for further processing, referred to as a "hybrid" approach to reverse logistics.

As the business and returns volume grows, omni-channel retailers and brands must think about whether it's time to open dedicated facilities to process returns or to co-locate returns processing in existing distribution centers; this decision depends on their company's particular needs.

Managing returns and customer orders in the same facility isn't easy, not to mention the fact that the cost to process returns is usually high, while the residual value of goods is usually low. That is why many omni-channel retailers outsource this process to 3PL providers who can focus on the efficient handling of returns and provide flexibility within the supply chain.

Third-party logistics (3PL) providers can design unique reverse logistics (RL) strategies to help their clients stay ahead of competition, as in most cases it is not an area of expertise for a company and the third party can do it more cheaply and efficiently. Insourcing or outsourcing is ultimately dependent on your business.

Reverse Logistics Technology

Not only is RL not typically a core competency of an omni-channel retailer, but they also have to develop or license RL-specific software to manage the process efficiently, which requires expertise and significant capital investment.

Luckily, there are now software systems built uniquely for RL which may provide a lower total cost of ownership and optimize long-term value. For most medium to large retailers and brands, buying an RL platform enables the company to continue focusing on its forward retail business.

Processing a return and repurposing, reconditioning, or recycling the goods can be costly in terms of time and cost to the merchant, resulting in reverse logistics potentially cutting profits by up to 20 percent per year.

To combat this, retailers can recoup a significant percentage of the total product cost by setting up a reverse logistics function with a 3PL provider who can resell the product, recycle it, or remanufacture it, so you don't have to [Lim, 2017].

One such example of this is shown in Case Study #2.

CASE STUDY #2: A HYBRID APPROACH TO OUTSOURCED REVERSE LOGISTICS

Best Buy [a major electronics retailer] [who] created a business unit ... to focus on developing sales of consumer electronics into the secondary markets ... No longer was the handling of customer returns, return to vendor and overstock a cost center sitting in a dark corner, but now it was transformed into a profit center ... at Best Buy, maximizing profit in the reverse logistics business is involving partnerships with both new and existing customers as well as manufacturers and third party service providers (3PSP's).

Online stores and Auctions – with product testing, inventory management, listing, payment collection and order fulfillment, Best Buy has built an integrated supply chain to take returned product from the stores and resell it to its value-seeking customers through eBay, a private online store and other online channels. Best Buy recently acquired Dealtree, its provider of these services.

Trade-in, an online program was launched in 2007, offering customers a fast and easy alternative to selling online themselves, or just letting working products sit in a drawer. It allows customers to recapture economic value, and through the Dealtree technology, Best Buy has instant access to current market value of products.

Refurbishment – working with a variety of 3PSP's, Best Buy has been integrating refurbished products into its warranty replacement program and selling direct to consumers.

Recycling – in 2008, Best Buy began testing offering free recycling in several markets. They have been building up a network of local certified recyclers and plan to roll nationwide in 2009 [Reverse Logistics Magazine Staff, 2009].

Whether using an insourced, outsourced, or a hybrid approach to managing the supply chain of your omni-channel business, a vast amount of collaboration is required, which is the topic of our next chapter.

14

The Importance of Collaboration and Visibility to the Omni-Channel Retail Supply Chain

The emergence of omni-channel retail has put a great deal of focus on and investment in engaging consumers, which has changed consumer expectations for delivery and service.

As omni-channel continues to grow and evolve, we are seeing a broadening in focus to include the back-end supply chain to enable and support those new expectations. The supply chain is at the very heart of profitability and service.

The key to enabling omni-channel retail is a supply chain that provides complete visibility of all inventory and investments, including goods that are in holding across all channels, in transit, or at consolidation points.

Retailers need to be lean and agile enough to identify all goods throughout the entire supply chain that are available to expedite, reroute, or allocate to consumers, while simultaneously understanding the cost and value of these decisions. This affects their processes, systems, and organizational structure.

However, in many ways, accomplishing this task profitably is easier said than done.

OMNI-CHANNEL GROWTH WILL DILUTE MARGINS UNLESS THE SUPPLY CHAIN CHANGES

Omni-channel can be a drag on profits according to an EY survey (2015) where only 38 percent said their omni-channel initiatives enhanced profits, while the rest said it either reduced profits or at best was neutral.

Therefore, where omni-channel drives growth but isn't profitable, margins are reduced, so it is critical that companies transform their operating models to make omni-channel effective for both the consumer and financial performance.

There are many reasons why companies have a hard time making omni-channel profitable. The pace of change and the urgency to sell products online have resulted in some bad decisions such as accepting poor terms, little or no visibility of how products are sold, and limited collaboration between manufacturers and retailers.

Additionally, in order to develop e-commerce capabilities, many companies have bolted on systems and processes without considering integration with traditional store fulfillment, resulting in inefficient supply chains with a lack of visibility across different channels.

Balancing Supply Chain Agility and Efficiency

Balancing efficiency and flexibility can be quite challenging as efficiency can mean that supply chains are less flexible and adaptable to a changing environment, including shrinking product cycles, volatile demand, and changing consumer behavior. To be successful, you need to have good planning, end-to-end visibility, and clear communication across channels and functional areas.

Additionally, the degree to which consumers expect efficiency over agility varies as some may want to click and collect the next day while many consumers don't need to get their order the next day.

So quicker isn't always better, as in some cases cost may be the defining factor, demanding efficiency, and in other cases, delivery speed may be the priority, requiring agility.

Seamless Data Visibility and Actionable Insight

Seamless omni-channel cannot be achieved by retailers or manufacturers alone, as it sometimes requires close collaboration between the two, and the constant sharing of information, as in the example of a manufacturer drop-shipping an order from a retailer directly to the consumer.

Seamless visibility isn't where it needs to be yet as retailers need more information from manufacturers than ever before. For example, retailers want more unstructured information, such as written copy for marketing or product images in a format they can easily leverage for digital channels.

Data Sharing Critical to Forecasting and Demand Sensing

Standardization and synchronization are important factors in improving supply chain efficiency as collaboration is key to closing the loop between the manufacturer and retailer, for example letting retailers know when they're continuing to order lines that are discontinued.

Collaboration in an online environment means working with the retailer where manufacturers and retailers regularly review products that have changed to make sure they are correct on the retailers' systems.

Standardization is important to improving supply chain efficiency by ensuring that all data are supplied in a consistent and uniform format. On the other hand, extreme standardization might not work for retailers that want to differentiate themselves as they may have unique needs to meet.

Furthermore, retailers must be willing to share relevant information with manufacturers which requires strong relationships as, for example, data sharing is important to forecasting and demand sensing (a forecasting method using mathematical techniques and near real-time information to create an accurate forecast of demand).

Leveraging Big Data

Traditional forecasting relied on historical data, but the trend towards collaborative forecasting has been "turbo-charged" as a result of omni-channel with the increasingly challenging nature of predicting which channel consumers will utilize (as well as any "cannibalization" of traditional channels not being used).

With the availability of big data and predictive analytics, companies are now able to make huge improvements in their demand-sensing capabilities. The movement of consumers using digital channels supplies increasingly rich data about their purchasing behavior and preferences. So, companies that can better utilize these data can gain significant benefits.

Analyzing these data effectively enables companies to ensure that they have a single view of the customer, and the right level of inventory in the right place, and that they can respond quickly to changing patterns of consumer demand, which today's consumer expects and demands.

In some cases, companies are combining consumer data with other information in real time. For example, some retailers and manufacturers are analyzing historical sales data along with meteorological information to see if the weather is heavily correlated with purchasing behavior. This can enable them to predict future demand for product lines more accurately by factoring the weather forecast into their production and inventory decisions.

Integrating IT and Supply Chain for Seamless Fulfillment

Better integration between information technology (IT) and the supply chain is critical for omni-channel success. However, according to a survey by EY (2015), only 26 percent of companies felt that they had effective IT systems and capabilities to enable seamless visibility and fulfillment to end consumers.

Even though lead times are constantly shortening, consumers expect the same level of inventory and service no matter the channel. So, companies must put in place an IT infrastructure that enables cross-channel visibility and the free flow of information across functional boundaries. Information silos still exist today and must be eliminated for cross-functional visibility and collaboration between product development, demand planning, logistics, and marketing.

It's hard to be agile if your ordering systems, for example, don't allow it. You need IT systems that support areas such as real-time predictive analytics, stock counting, and ordering, and you need the technology to make that happen.

Requirements for Success

In order to enable your supply chain to have the agility, visibility, and efficiency required to profitably support omni-channel retail, you need to focus on the following:

Strategy

- Focus on the needs of the consumer and don't over-engineer omni-channel.
- Dedicate resources to prioritize omni-channel and collaborate across channels to remove silo behavior.

- Prioritize a continuous improvement mindset to keep up with fast-changing technology platforms and behaviors.
- Design products and packaging for the requirements of omni-channel.

Agility

- Plan for supply chain needs of the future, or you risk always being behind.
- Segment the supply chain to meet the different product and channel demands.
- Utilize existing assets, where possible, in a creative way to support the omni-channel need.
- Make (and perfect) "click-and-collect" as a priority over home delivery.

Visibility

- Incentivize data sharing to obtain an end-to-end view of the value chain.
- Move past traditional sales forecasting to sense and shape demand.
- Use your data to create a single view of the customer across all channels (including returns).
- Leverage advanced analytics platforms to drive detail on "cost to serve" to better understand profit drivers [EY, 2015a].

DIFFERENCES BETWEEN OMNI-CHANNEL AND OMNI-CHANNEL 2.0

As opposed to the original definition of omni-channel, omni-channel 2.0 is about bringing the entire enterprise together, not just enabling support within legacy systems for an omni-channel approach. Retailers and supply chain leaders need to increase integration and visibility across all channels, engaging with consumers and personalizing the shopping experience. In omni-channel 2.0, you know who the customer is throughout the process; you know what the customer is looking for and what the next best action is for the customer.

What Is Omni-Channel 2.0, and How Is It Different from the Original Omni-Channel?

Traditional omni-channel, also known as "original omni-channel", is the combining of supply chain channels allowing customers to shop from any channel seamlessly.

This required supply chains to integrate storefronts, distribution centers, and online ordering processes into an overarching platform which hasn't always occurred, as disruptions in the customer experience continued to exist.

Instead of an overarching, flexible platform, many retailers have continued to use legacy systems through custom interfaces that lead to inefficiencies and integration problems.

Omni-channel 2.0 refers to retailers and supply chain leaders increasing their proficiency across all channels (not just being "present"), engaging with consumers, and personalizing the shopping experience, enabling them to eliminate barriers to new technology implementation, offering better customer service, and being ready for the next innovation.

In summary, the goal of omni-channel 2.0 is to break down silos and bring the entire enterprise together (i.e. people, process, and technology) through a more open-platform approach, not just enabling support within legacy systems for an omni-channel approach.

Benefits of Omni-Channel 2.0

Omni-channel 2.0 has many benefits for consumers and retailers, including flexible fulfillment options across multiple channels, end-to-end visibility, improved inventory management, fewer occurrences of overstocking and under stocking, and improved IT processes and integration between systems.

How to Move toward Omni-Channel 2.0

Retailers and warehouses must work to satisfy more and more customers, stay competitive, and create a unique customer experience.

If companies don't embrace omni-channel 2.0, they risk losing any chance for a sustained competitive advantage with higher overhead, and employee turnover rates.

Some ways to fully utilize omni-channel 2.0 in retail include:

Integrate and increase vendor base – Supply chain executives should begin the process by integrating existing systems and expanding their vendor base, allowing companies to exploit the value of newer, more adaptable, and flexible supply chain systems.

Break omni-channel 2.0 implementation into steps – As rapid change across an entire enterprise can lead to disruptions, rather than applying all omni-channel 2.0 processes at once, supply chain leaders should focus on incremental changes.

Develop and maintain a customer-centric strategy – Customer-centricity is a foundation of omni-channel 2.0. Using a high-cost model of trying to meet omni-channel standards with legacy systems is a recipe for failure in the long run. As stated earlier, not many retailers can fulfill omni-channel demand profitably, so investments into omni-channel should focus on improving profitability and meeting growing customer demands.

Engage with customers to obtain feedback – Customer expectations, especially through feedback, will continue to evolve as retailers offer new, exciting services as part of the omni-channel 2.0 development trend. This can allow a retailer to differentiate themselves by interacting with customers to find out what they can do better to provide a better customer experience.

Take Advantage of Omni-Channel 2.0

Omni-channel 2.0 is not just a "prediction", it is the recipe for a sustained competitive advantage, as retailers and their supply chains need to continuously improve since customers today want their products now, from any ordering portal, and the ability to pick up online orders from in-store locations, and to have another piece shipped to their home, while still having the option of getting notifications on their phones when they enter a store about items on sale.

This requires integrated comprehensive systems with increased flexibility and productivity with limited resources [Rosing, 2019].

HOW TO GAIN VISIBILITY ACROSS THE EXTENDED SUPPLY CHAIN THROUGH EVERY SELLING CHANNEL

As mentioned, retailers are finding it hard to meet customer expectations across all channels at least in part due to lack of end-to-end inventory visibility.

The power has shifted to buyers in the retail market today, and they want more options and often leverage retailers against each other due to the Internet's transparency to get the best value for their money. While retailers want to meet consumer demand, most don't have a system that can bring all inventory data onto a single platform. This makes it hard to see where their products are and to provide accurate information to buyers. In general, this causes inventory of the same items to be isolated in each selling channel and, as a result, retailers end up relying on buffer inventory while delivering lower levels of customer service.

Impact of Poor Omni-Channel Visibility

In the event that retailers can't see their inventory across all selling channels, they may miss out on opportunities to sell and gain customer loyalty. Some negative aspects of this include:

- Inaccurate inventory and lack of visibility create the need for excess inventory to protect the sale.
- Lack of integrated systems reduces cross-channel visibility and the effective use of inventory.
- Lack of extended supply chain visibility from the manufacturer, including planning, purchasing, and factory floor to goods in-transit, makes it difficult for retailers to promise accurate availability dates.

The Root Cause of the Problem

There are a number of activities that can create the need for omni-channel visibility. They include:

1. Increasing consumer expectations – Today's customers expect to buy a product at a time, place, and price that works for them. If goods are out of stock or delivered late, they may consider switching to a different retailer which may lead to additional lost sales and lower revenue from fewer purchases and more markdowns.
2. Expanding global reach in supply chains – Retailers are sourcing and selling in new markets domestically and overseas, sending products to stores and directly to customers who order online. So, it's no surprise that the more regions involved in a supply chain, the easier it is to lose track of inventory, which can result in a higher

landed cost of product, excess and shortages of inventory due to poor allocation, and barriers to entry in new markets.

3. Technological advances – Leading-edge technology can blur the lines between commerce and e-commerce by allowing customers to purchase in a variety of ways such as mobile phones, tablets, in-store from kiosks that pull from online inventory, and online to pick up at a store later. The cross-channel demand that results can cause confusion up the supply chain, causing expensive expedited air freight and the over-promising and under-delivering on product availability.

Heading in the Right Direction

Retailers are investing a lot of money into new technology to gain visibility, manage data, and collaborate with their global trading partners.

One option available is to use a cloud-based system, where retailers can provide customers and themselves with a view of all inventory, no matter which channel is being used. An advantage of an integrated cloud system is that it can automatically allocate from a single pool of inventory when an order is made, regardless of where the customer is viewing the product.

Other goals offering potential competitive advantages of an integrated omni-channel platform (installed or cloud-based) are to:

- Gain visibility across the extended supply chain at the most granular level possible.
- Combine data from partners (ERP, factory, forwarder, carrier, bank).
- Gain inventory visibility and availability of item/SKU from production to consumer.
- Accurately promise delivery dates and respond to changing customer demand.

An omni-channel platform solution should also be able to help you:

1. Collaborate with your supply chain partners to find in-transit inventory status.
2. Adjust volumes and dynamically allocate based on changing customer demand.
3. Adjust manufacturing to produce and deploy (or not) SKUs that are over-selling or under-selling.

Value Proposition

By viewing all inventory in one integrated platform, retailers can greatly improve customer service (Figure 14.1).

To recap, the benefits from improved omni-channel visibility can help omni-channel companies to:

1. Obtain higher fill rates and reduce stockouts by using accurate item-level details to locate items and create dynamic ETAs from shipment notifications and milestones and count in-transit inventory as on-hand for any channel.
2. Reduce markdowns and the need for buffer inventory to increase margins by allocating to demand and lowering inventory costs.
3. Increase service levels and customer satisfaction by having your products in stock at the right place and right time [GTNEXUS, 2017].

In summary, to improve omni-channel visibility, companies must transform themselves from silo-based, inward-facing corporate operators to interconnected, lean, and agile supply chain network collaborators, the topic of our next chapter.

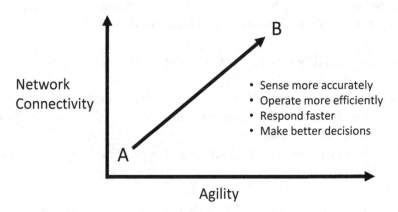

FIGURE 14.1
Omni-channel and the networked company.

15

A Lean and Agile Supply Chain for Retail, Wholesale, and Manufacturing to Keep up with the Omni-Channel World

In today's global, dynamic economy with a "buy anywhere, fulfill anywhere" omni-channel ideology in the retail marketplace, it is beneficial for companies to operate a supply chain that is both lean and agile. Using lean and agile in combination is known as having a hybrid supply chain strategy.

HYBRID SUPPLY CHAIN

A hybrid supply chain strategy may be appropriate for a company attempting to become a "mass customizer" – producing progressively smaller batch sizes (sometimes as little as one item) specific to customers' sometimes unique needs.

A lean supply chain focuses on adding value for customers, while identifying and eliminating waste – anything that doesn't add that value, often through the standardization of processes and systems (e.g. SOPs and ERP systems). Being agile and responsive, on the other hand, implies that your supply chain can handle unpredictability – and a constant stream of new, innovative products – with speed and flexibility.

An agile strategy uses a wait-and-see approach to customer demand by not committing to the final product until actual demand becomes known (also referred to as postponement). For example, this might involve the subassembly of components into modules in a lower-cost process, with final assembly done close to the point of demand in order to localize the product.

An agile supply chain must be responsive to actual demand, and capable of using information as a substitute (to some degree) for inventory through collaboration and integration with key customers and suppliers.

Either or Both

On some occasions, either an agile or a lean strategy might be appropriate for a supply chain. But many companies will probably face situations where a hybrid strategy is a better fit. If so, they need to carefully plan and execute the combined strategy with excellence, which is often easier said than done because it involves a lot of moving parts. As in so many aspects of supply chain and operations management, there is more than one way to accomplish this goal.

One example of a company using a hybrid strategy in its supply chain is Zara, a Spanish fashion designer and retailer. Zara directly manufactures most of the products it designs and sells, and performs activities such as cutting, dying, labeling, and packaging in-house to gain economies of scale. A network of dedicated subcontractors performs other finishing operations that cannot be completed in-house.

As a result, Zara has a supply chain that is not only agile and flexible, but incorporates many lean characteristics into its processes.

Some semiconductor manufacturers incorporate a hybrid strategy using a flexible manufacturing and distribution model. Subcontractors perform distinct manufacturing processes at separate physical locations. This hybrid approach taps a virtual network of manufacturing partners and requires responsive, flexible, and information-driven sourcing, manufacturing, and distribution functions – in many ways, the opposite of Zara's strategy of shifting processes in-house.

Many organizations can find some form of hybrid supply chain that works well for them. In today's ever-changing, volatile, and competitive global economy, it may often be in a company's best interest to operate a supply chain that is both lean and agile [Myerson, 2014].

In order to implement this philosophy with its rather unique culture in today's omni-channel retail environment, you first need to understand what it's all about.

HISTORY OF LEAN

Early concepts like *labor specialization* (Smith), where an individual was responsible for a single repeatable activity, and *standardized parts* (Whitney) helped to improve efficiency and quality (Figure 15.1).

At the turn of the 20th century, the era of scientific management arrived where concepts such as *time and motion studies* (Taylor) and *Gantt charts* (Gantt) allowed management to measure, analyze, and manage activities much more precisely.

During the early 1900s the era of mass production arrived. Concepts like the assembly line, economies of scale (producing large quantities of the same item to spread fixed costs), and statistical sampling were utilized. Today this is referred to as a "push" process, which is the opposite of "demand pull" (by the customer) used in a lean philosophy.

Lean, originally applied to the manufacturing industry, was developed by the Japanese automotive industry, largely Toyota, while re-building the Japanese economy after World War II. Material was scarce, and they realized that in order to compete with the U.S. auto companies they would have to work smarter.

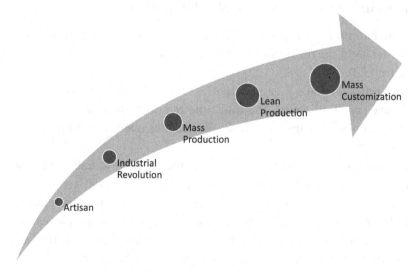

FIGURE 15.1
History of lean.

The concept of lean was little known outside Japan until the 1970s (generally known as "JIT" as the actual term "lean" didn't come about until the 1990s). England had early experience with lean manufacturing from the Japanese automotive plants in the U.K.

Up until the 1990s only the automotive industry had adopted lean manufacturing and that was primarily on the shop floor. Since then it has spread into aerospace and general manufacturing, consumer electronics, healthcare, construction, and, more recently, to food manufacturing and meat processing as well as to other processes such as the administrative and support functions as well as the supply chain.

In today's global economy, companies source product and material world-wide, looking for the best quality at the lowest cost. E-commerce and enterprise resource planning (ERP) systems have made for easy entry to the global economy for smaller companies as well, allowing them to compete against much larger competitors.

This has led to the concept of "mass customization", which is the ability to combine the low per-unit costs of mass production with the flexibility associated with individual customization (e.g. Dell which can configure, assemble, test, and ship your customized order within 24 hours).

Value-Added vs. Non-Value-Added Activities

In order to understand the lean concept of "waste", it is first important to understand the meaning of value-added vs. non-value-added activities (Figure 15.2).

Any process entails a set of activities. The activities in total are known as "cycle" or "lead time". The lead time required for a product to move through a process from start to finish includes queues/waiting time and processing time.

The individual activities or work elements that actually transform inputs (e.g. raw materials) to outputs (e.g. finished goods) are known as "processing" time. In general, processing adds value from the customer's standpoint. Processing time is the time that it takes an employee to go through all of their work elements before repeating them. It is measured from the beginning of a process step to the end of that process step.

If we think of a simple example such as taking raw lumber and making it into a pallet of 2 × 4s, the value added for the customer is the actual processing that transforms the raw lumber into the final pallet of 2 × 4s.

FIGURE 15.2
Value-added vs. non-value-added activities.

This would include activities such as washing, trimming, cutting, etc., and is a relatively small part of the cycle time (i.e. it may only take one hour to process the raw material into a finished pallet, but the entire cycle time may be one week).

In lean terms, the non-value-added time is actually much greater than just the lead time. We include current inventory "on the floor" (i.e. raw, WIP, and finished goods) and, using a calculated takt time for a specific "value stream" (a single or family of products or services which will be discussed later in this chapter), convert those quantities to days of supply. Doing so can expand the non-value-added time from days to weeks (or even months).

It is very common for many processes (or value streams) to only have 5–10 percent value-added activities. However, there are some necessary non-value-added activities such as regulatory, customer requirements, and legal requirements that, as they don't add value, are waste. As they are necessary, we can't eliminate them, but we should try to apply them as efficiently as is possible.

174 • Omni-Channel Retail Supply Chain

It is fairly normal for management to focus primarily on speeding up processes, often value-added ones such as the stamping speed on a press. From a lean perspective, the focus moves to non-value-added activities, which in some cases may even result in slowing down the entire process in order to balance it, remove bottlenecks, and increase flow.

WASTE

In lean terms, non-value-added activities are referred to as "waste". Typically, when a product or information is being stored, inspected or delayed, waiting in line, or defective, it is not adding value and is 100 percent waste.

These wastes can be found in any process, whether it's manufacturing, administrative, supply chain and logistics, or elsewhere in your organization.

Below are listed the eight wastes. One easy way to remember them is that they spell "TIM WOODS" (Figure 15.3):

Transportation – Excessive movement of people, products, and information.

Inventory – Storing material or documentation ahead of requirements. Excess inventory often covers for variations in processes as a result of high scrap or rework levels, long setup times, late deliveries, process downtime, and quality problems.

Motion – Unnecessary bending, turning, reaching, and lifting.

Waiting – For parts, information, instructions, equipment.

Overproduction – Making more than is immediately required.

Over-processing – Tighter tolerances or higher-grade materials than are necessary.

Defects – Rework, scrap, and incorrect documentation (i.e. errors).

Skills – Underutilizing capabilities of employees, delegating tasks with inadequate training.

There are a variety of places to look for waste in your supply chain and logistics function.

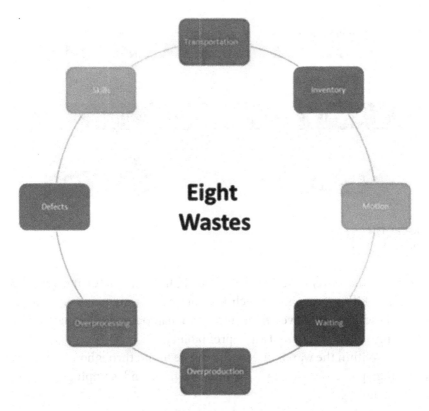

FIGURE 15.3
The eight wastes.

One way to consider where waste might exist in the supply chain is in terms of the SCOR model (Figure 15.4):

Plan – It all starts (and ends) with a solid sales and operations planning (S&OP) process (or lack thereof). If there isn't one in an organization, then there is probably plenty of waste in the supply chain.

Source – As purchasing accounts for approximately 50 percent (or more) of the total expenditures, using sound procurement approaches discussed earlier in this book such as EOQ and the use of JIT principles (including vendor-managed inventory (VMI)) can go a long way towards reducing waste, especially excess inventory. Partnerships, collaborations, and joint reviews with suppliers can also help to identify and reduce waste.

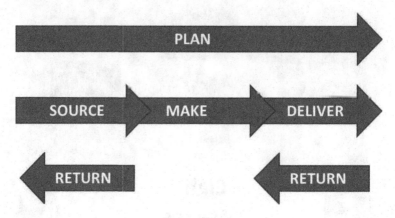

FIGURE 15.4
The SCOR model.

Make (and store) – Activities such as (light) manufacturing, assembly, and kitting, much of which is done in the warehouse or by a 3PL these days, can have a huge impact on material and information flow, impacting productivity and profitability.

Within the warehouse, waste can be found throughout the receiving, put away, storage, picking, staging, and shipping processes including:

- Defective products which create returns.
- Overproduction or over-shipment of products.
- Excess inventories which require additional space and reduce warehousing efficiency.
- Excess motion and handling.
- Inefficiencies and unnecessary processing steps.
- Transportation steps and distances.
- Waiting for parts, materials, and information.
- Information processes.

Each step in the warehousing process should be examined critically to see where unnecessary, repetitive, and non-value-added activities might be, so that they may be eliminated.

Deliver – Transportation optimization (especially important with high fuel prices). This would include routing, scheduling, and maintenance among other things.

Return – Shipping mistakes, returns, product quality, and warranty issues often ignored or an afterthought.

Enable – Added in version 11 of the SCOR model in 2012, this includes processes associated with the management of the supply chain. These processes include the management of business rules, performance, data, resources, facilities, contracts, supply chain network management, managing regulatory compliance, and risk management. It is not only important to just say you have these processes, but you must also have implemented them efficiently so that they are tied to the lean goals of the organization and, as a result, you can ensure that you are meeting these goals and objectives.

There are a variety of lean tools available which we will discuss briefly in this chapter. However, it is most important to first have a lean culture and support that is conducive to success, as lean is more of a journey than any individual project.

LEAN CULTURE AND TEAMWORK

In order to be successful for the long term, any type of program has some key success factors (KSFs). In the case of lean, they include:

- Train the entire organization and make sure everyone understands the lean philosophy and understand that it may be a cultural change for the organization.
- Ensure that top management actively drives and supports the change with strong leadership.
- Everyone in the organization should commit to make it work.
- Find a good, experienced change agent as the "champion".
- Set a kaizen (i.e. continuous improvement project) agenda and communicate it and involve operators through empowered teams.
- Map value streams, apply lean tools, and begin as soon as possible with an important and visible activity.
- Integrate the supporting functions and build internal customer and supplier relationships.

Lean Teams

Teamwork is essential for competing in today's global arena, where individual perfection is not as desirable as a high level of collective performance.

In knowledge-based enterprises, teams are the norm rather than the exception. A critical feature of these teams is that they have a significant degree of empowerment, or decision-making authority.

There are many different kinds of teams: Top management teams, focused task forces, self-directed teams, concurrent engineering teams, product/service development and/or launch teams, quality improvement teams, and so on.

It is no different in lean. As a result, it is important to establish lean teams that can develop a systematic process that consistently defines and solves problems utilizing lean tools.

Lean teams are a great way to share ideas and create a support system, helping to ensure better "buy in" for the implementation of improvements.

Successful teams realize the "power of teamwork" and teamwork culture and that the goal is more important than anyone's individual role. However, teams must be in a "risk-free" environment but have leadership, discipline, trust, and the tools and training to make things happen.

To make teamwork happen, it is important that executive leaders communicate the clear expectation that teamwork and collaboration are expected and that the organization members talk about and identify the value of a teamwork culture. Teamwork should be rewarded and recognized, and important stories and folklore that people discuss within the company should emphasize teamwork.

Kaizen and Teams

The word "kaizen", which literally means "improvement" in Japanese, refers to activities that continually improve all functions and involve all employees.

Kaizen events are a big part of a successful lean program. A typical kaizen event involves a team of people for a period of 3–10 days. They typically focus on a working (or proposed) process with the goal of a rapid, dramatic performance improvement. Typically, the event starts with training on the topic of the event to ensure common understanding.

Team and Kaizen Objectives

Once teams have been established and basic training has begun to start a lean philosophy, it is important for any projects undertaken by teams to have proper objectives to ensure success. So, you will need to ask questions such as:

- What is the customer telling you in terms of the cost, service, and quality of your products/services?
- What objectives and goals have been established by your company to address market needs?
- What processes immediately impact the performance of these products and services?
- Who needs to support this effort?
- How can the business objectives be used to garner support?

By asking these types of questions, it's not hard to link lean projects to overall and functional objectives and metrics for improvement.

VALUE STREAM MAPPING (VSM)

Before discussing specific lean tools, it is first important to understand the current processes to be examined. Lean has a visual, relatively high- and broad-level method for analyzing a current state and designing a future state for the series of activities (both value-added and non-value-added) required to produce a single or family of products or services for a customer, known as a "value stream map" (VSM).

A VSM is typically labeled a "paper and pencil" tool, although it may be constructed digitally and is a value management tool designed to create two separate visual representations (i.e. "maps").

The *first map* illustrates how data and resources move through the "value stream" during the production process, and is used to identify wastes, defects, and failures (Figure 15.5); the *second map*, using data contained in the first, illustrates a "future state map" of the same value stream with any waste, defects, and failures eliminated (Figure 15.6).

The two maps are used to create detailed strategic and implementation plans to enhance the value stream's performance.

A VSM is usually one of the first steps your company should take in creating an overall lean initiative plan.

Developing a visual map of the value stream allows everyone to fully understand and agree on how value is produced and where waste occurs.

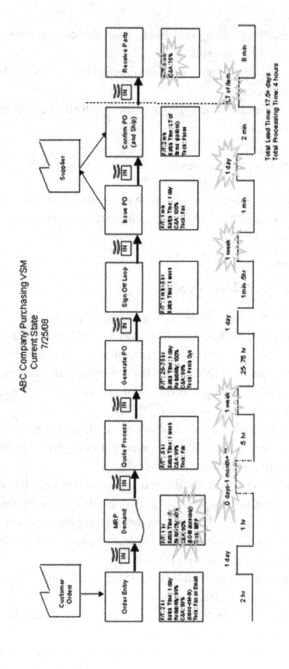

FIGURE 15.5

Current state value stream map.

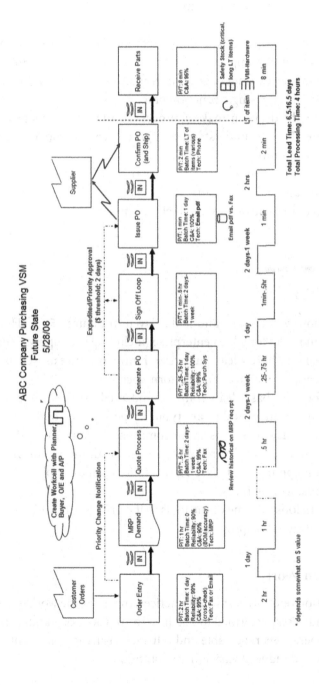

FIGURE 15.6

Future state value stream map.

VSM Benefits

Benefits of value stream mapping include:

- Highlights connections among activities and information and material flow that impact the lead time of your value stream.
- Helps employees understand your company's entire value stream rather than just a single function of it.
- Improves the decision-making process of all work teams by helping team members to understand and accept your company's current practices and future plans.
- Allows you to separate value-added activities from non-value-added activities and then measure their lead time. Provides a way for employees to easily identify and eliminate areas of waste.

LEAN TOOLS

As was previously discussed and is displayed in Figure 15.7's "House of lean", the foundation for a lean enterprise (including the supply chain and logistics areas) is to have a lean culture and infrastructure as well as a way to set and measure objectives and performance.

After performing basic lean training and establishing teams, one or more value stream map studies are typically performed to identify areas for improvement. However, it is not uncommon for teams to "brainstorm" to come up with ideas for future kaizen events in addition to or instead of value stream mapping events (see Figure 15.8 for an example of a kaizen form for brainstorming ideas).

Next, we will look at some of the tools that can be used by lean teams in pursuit of continuous improvement.

Standardized Work

Standardization refers to best work practices, that is, as the work is actually routinely (and best) performed in real life. The purpose of standardization is to make operations repeatable and reliable, ensuring consistently high productivity, and reduced variability of output.

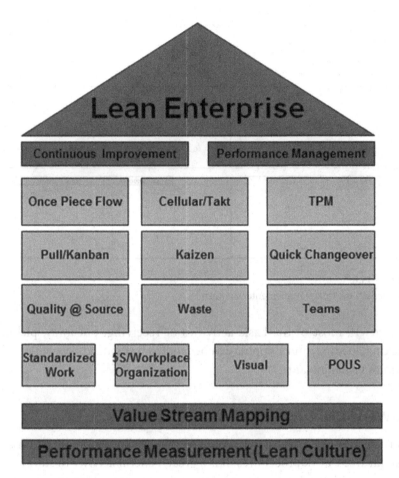

FIGURE 15.7
House of lean.

It ensures that all activities are safely carried out, with all tasks organized in the best-known sequence using the most effective combination of people, material, machines, and methods.

It is important, where possible, to make standard work more of a "visual job aid" that is easy to understand and follow (e.g. a laminated simplified list of standard instructions supplemented with digital photographs).

In the supply chain and logistics function, standardized work (preferably visual) can be applied nearly everywhere. The office and warehouse are the most common places where standardized work can be found, and can include order processing, invoicing, and drawings. Out on the warehouse

Cost Reduction Kaizen Implementation

Department: _____	Process for Kaizen:_____		Kaizen #: _____
Cost Center: _____			Date: _____
Approvals: Lean Champion: ____	Maint: ____	Controller: ____	GM: ____

1) Current Situation	3) Solution Activity	

2) Analysis	4) Cost Reduction	(Total Savings:)
	Current	Proposed

FIGURE 15.8

Cost reduction kaizen implementation form.

floor itself, most of the basic activities of receiving, put away, picking, packing, loading, and shipping can benefit from standardized work in the form of visual job aids.

5S-Workplace Organization System

5S is a philosophy that focuses on effective workplace organization and standardized work procedures. It is a great, general activity to start a lean program with, as it's easy to understand and implement throughout a business.

5S simplifies your work environment, and reduces waste and non-value activity while improving quality efficiency and safety. It ensures that the workplace is clean, organized, orderly, safe, efficient, and pleasant, resulting in:

- Fewer accidents
- Improved efficiency
- Reduced searching time
- Reduced contamination
- Visual workplace control
- A foundation for all other improvement activities

A 5S project begins with the selection of a specific area (usually one that is fairly disorganized) and a multi-functional team that includes at least one member from the selected area.

Next, the team goes to the selected area to perform a "workplace scan" which involves activities such as taking "before" pictures, drawing a "spaghetti diagram" showing locations of materials and equipment as well as product flow, and the performance of some kind of 5S audit (various forms are readily available on the Internet).

The steps in 5S (and what the actual "S"s stand for) are:

Sort – Unneeded items are identified and removed. Only needed parts, tools, and instructions remain.

Set in order – Everything has a place; everything is in its place. Create visual controls to know where items belong and when they are missing, as well as how much to keep on-hand in the area.

Shine – Do an initial spring cleaning. This can include scouring as well as some painting.

Standardize – Routine cleaning becomes a way of life. Preventative maintenance is routinely performed. Standards are created to maintain the first three Ss.

Sustain – This is perhaps the hardest part of 5S, where it has to become a routine way of life. Root causes are routinely identified and dealt with.

Visual Controls

Simple visual signals give the operator the information to make the right decision. They are efficient, self-regulating, and worker-managed.

Examples include visual job aids mentioned previously, kanbans, "andon" lights (i.e. green = process working; red = process stopped), color-coded dies, tools, pallets, and lines on the floor to delineate storage areas, walkways, work areas, etc.

Facility Layout

Considering optimal facility layout, like standardized work, is nothing new. However, as a tool of lean it is focused primarily on maximizing flow and eliminating wastes such as transportation and motion. If used properly it can result in:

- Higher utilization of space, equipment, and people.
- Improved flow of information, materials, or people.
- Improved employee morale.
- Improved customer/client interface.
- Increased flexibility.

Batch Size Reduction and Quick Changeover

The concepts of batch size reduction and quick changeover (sometimes also referred to as "setup reduction") are highly intertwined.

When material is "pushed" through a supply chain and operations process, you produce, store, and ship in large quantities to spread your fixed costs among a large number of items, thus minimizing your costs per unit. In "pull", you schedule what the downstream customer actually wants, using a just-in-time (JIT) approach. The goal is one-piece flow (or at least a reduction in batch or lot size).

Long changeovers tend to create larger batch sizes, resulting in higher inventory costs, longer lead times, and potentially larger quality issues, and that is why we focus on reducing changeover times though "setup reduction" kaizen events.

In supply chain and logistics processes, we often see the results of batching in production to cover manufacturing wastes that result in excess inventory, and in purchasing to obtain economies of scale. Additionally, there is a large amount of batching of paperwork in the office, which, if reduced, can encourage improved flow and getting orders out faster, resulting in a shorter order-to-cash cycle.

In warehouse operations, there are setups everywhere, including receiving, picking, staging, loading, and shipping (especially during shift start-ups).

Quality at the Source

Also known as "source control", the idea with this concept is that the next step in the process is your customer and, as a result, you need to ensure a perfect product for your customer.

One major technique used in source control is known as "poka-yoke" which is the concept of using foolproof devices or techniques designed to pass only acceptable product. Poka-yokes can range from simple tools, such as a "cut out" to ensure proper dimensions, to a scale at a packing station that checks the weight of an item and, if it is outside of the proper range, software would prevent a label from printing.

Quality at the source can eliminate or reduce final inspections, reduce passed-on defects, eliminate non-value-added processing, increase throughput, and increase employee satisfaction.

Quality at the source helps to reduce the total cost of quality, which highlights the true impact of defective work as it moves towards the customer. This includes:

- Prevention costs – Reducing the potential for defects (e.g. poka-yokes).
- Appraisal costs – Evaluating products, parts, and services (e.g. quality control sampling).
- Internal failure – Producing defective parts or service before delivery (e.g. final inspection).
- External costs – Defects discovered after delivery (e.g. returns).

Obviously, the further along a quality issue gets, the greater the impact (cost and otherwise) it has on an organization.

Other techniques such as standardized work, visual workplace, and 5S are all tools for implementing quality at the source.

Point of Use Storage

Point of use storage is the storing of raw materials and supplies nearby the work area that will use them. It works best if the supplier can deliver frequent, on-time, small deliveries. It can simplify the physical inventory tracking, storage, and handling processes.

Total Productive Maintenance (TPM)

Total productive maintenance (TPM) is often used interchangeably with the concept of preventative maintenance. While preventative maintenance may be involved, TPM is actually a team-based systematic approach to the elimination of equipment-related waste. It involves the charting and analysis of equipment performance to identify the root cause of problems, and then the implementation of permanent corrective actions.

TPM is a shared responsibility, which involves not only mechanics but operators, engineers, and employees from other functional areas.

Ultimately, in addition to creating "counter measures" using techniques such as poka-yokes, TPM develops preventive maintenance plans that utilize the best practices of operators, maintenance departments, and depot service. It also involves the training of workers to operate and maintain their own machines, often referred to as "autonomous maintenance".

While the supply chain and logistics function may not have as much or as complicated equipment as in manufacturing, there is plenty of equipment that must run at peak performance, including forklifts and carousels in a warehouse, trucks on the road, and office equipment including computer hardware and software.

Pull/Kanban and Work Cells

As mentioned before, a "push" system produces product, using forecasts or schedules, without regard for what is needed by the next operation, whereas a "pull" system is a method of controlling the flow of resources by indirectly linking dissimilar functions, through the use of visual controls (e.g. kanbans), replacing only what has been consumed at the demand rate of the customer.

A pull system is a flexible and simple method of controlling and balancing the flow of resources and eliminates the waste of handling, storage, expediting, obsolescence, rework, facilities, equipment, and excess paperwork. It consists of processing based on actual consumption, planned work in process (paperwork), and management by sight, with improved communication.

One of the main tools in a pull system is a kanban, in which a user removes a standard-sized container and a signal is seen by the producing/ supplying department as authorization to replenish. The signal can be a card or even something as simple as a line on a wall.

Another lean tool is known as a "work cell", which reorganizes people and machines that typically would be dispersed in various departments into a group so that they can focus on making a single product or a group of related items. Work cells are usually "U"-shaped vs. a traditional linear assembly line type of format.

Work cells require the identification of families of products or services and require a high level of training and flexibility on the part of employees, and in many cases utilize poka-yokes at each station in the cell.

Work cells can be found on the shop floor, in a warehouse, and the office, in a variety of industries. In the warehouse, there may be more limited opportunities than elsewhere, but they are typically found in areas such as packaging or in value-added activities performed by 3PLs, such as the packaging of kits for a customer, or in a staging location to organize outgoing shipments.

Lean and Six Sigma

In recent years, lean has often been combined with Six Sigma to become "Lean Six Sigma" in many companies. The concept of Six Sigma was originated by Motorola in the early 1980s and is now used in many industries. Six Sigma attempts to improve the quality of process outputs by identifying and removing the causes of defects (errors) and minimizing variability in manufacturing and business processes, thus the term "Six Sigma" which refers to a process which has 99.99966 percent of products produced free of defects.

Lean and Six Sigma are complementary as lean uses relatively simple concepts to make improvements and covers the *entire* process or value stream, beginning with the customer end and going upstream to suppliers, and Six Sigma is a tool (heavily statistical) that looks at individual steps in the process and attempts to identify and remove defects and variability. In general, lean tries to reduce waste in the production process, and Six Sigma tries to add value to the production process [Myerson, 2012].

Needless to say, lean retail thrives in an omni-channel world, by helping streamline a business's retail operations in order to expediently provide excellent goods and services, while maximizing value for the customer.

OMNI-CHANNEL REQUIRES AN AGILE AND RESPONSIVE SUPPLY CHAIN

While lean can improve quality and productivity, and reduce waste and cost, an agile and responsive supply chain is also important in an omni-channel environment, as the customer controls not just what to buy, but also the when, where, and how.

The demand to re-configure centers has evolved into demand for the creation of facilities that can handle retail, wholesale, and direct-to-consumer in the same location, pulling from the same inventory.

The changes affect the entire organization – facilities, equipment, technology, and people – and agility is critical to supporting omni-channel requirements because the environment is constantly changing.

Because of this, the key to achieving an agile supply chain in an omni-channel world is orchestration: Having the technology and systems in place to move products through the supply chain seamlessly while still being in control at the origin.

Key supply chain challenges are dynamic demand across channels, high shipping costs, and costs associated with different fulfillment types. These factors add to the complexity in the supply chain process, and also impact the lead time and the cost of serving the customer.

THE RETAIL SUPPLY CHAIN NEEDS TO CONTINUOUSLY ADAPT

Omni-channel retail is putting a lot of pressure on the supply chain. Retailers need to provide multiple delivery options to multiple destinations, deliver accurately and on time, and be affordable.

The retail supply chain is made up of the processes used to get your products to your consumers and ranges from procuring raw materials to make your product, to delivering that product into your consumers' hands. Retail supply chain management then focuses on the need to optimize those processes to maximize both speed and efficiency.

Areas for Change and Improvement

Some areas where you can usually reduce costs are improving your distribution and fulfillment strategy and operations, improving supplier relationships, analyzing customer demand patterns, and turning product faster. This enables retailers to offer lower prices and a better customer experience for a competitive advantage.

It is estimated that the cost of out-of-stocks and overstocks among retailers today, if eliminated, could increase same-store sales by 9.2 percent (not an easy task, for sure).

One benefit of the growth of e-commerce is that it has enabled retailers to sell to consumers anywhere in the world. However, there are still geographic constraints on the logistics and fulfillment of supply. Supply can still be restricted because of the costs that come with buying and holding inventory.

With consumer-facing omni-channel retailing, it is important to provide flexibility for your items to be purchased at a store, on the Web, or on mobile devices, but great technology won't help much if you don't have a supply chain geared for quick and efficient order fulfillment.

Therefore, supply-side innovation, control, and flexibility are the key to winning, as seen by Amazon and Walmart.

For small to mid-sized retailers to endure, inventory flow needs to change from a mostly product "push" process based upon forecasts to more of a product pull and reactive supply chain with the kind of agility that has been successful for Amazon and Walmart.

As we know, consumers love having an assortment of choices which requires a commitment to optimizing logistics and investing in technology, resulting in a wider assortment of products that may reduce inventory risk. To accomplish this without escalating costs, many retailers have adopted management philosophies such as a lean and agile supply chain along with techniques such as drop-shipping, postponement, lean enterprise, and JIT.

Some key benefits and competitive advantages provided by this streamlined, flexible pull approach are:

Endless aisle – This term refers to the retailer's ability to sell out-of-stock items to in-store customers or sell online items that are not kept in local inventory. By matching supply and demand in real time, you assist consumers in accessing what they want, where they want, and from whom they want. That results in selling more products, in more places, more accurately.

Competitive pricing – More than ever, to succeed you need competitive pricing. Increased visibility of products in your supply chain also helps reduce prices of products by bringing down overhead and fulfillment costs.

Reduced costs – Increasing selling opportunities does not have to result in increased transportation and storage costs. For example, Amazon doesn't have to pay for third-party inventory that it moves through its distribution hubs, as the only cost Amazon incurs when providing third-party fulfillment is money they would have spent on the infrastructure, labor, transportation, and other direct sales operation costs anyway.

Another example can be found with Ocado, the British e-commerce firm that is the world's largest online-only grocery chain, and operates 1,100 robots that process 65,000 customer orders per week at their Hampshire, England, warehouse.

Ocado has maximized their supply chain efficiencies to deliver product rapidly at the lowest possible cost. Ocado has three automated warehouses, one of which turns more than $1.2 billion a year and another which turns $1.4 billion a year. Their three automated warehouses individually pick 1.5 million items a day with over 99 percent item accuracy in their orders. Ocado promises its customers that its prices will be cheaper than its huge competitor Tesco, partially as a result of the efficiencies provided by automation, which has supported accuracy and reduced costs. It has also optimized the routing of its deliveries, resulting in a typical Ocado van having annual sales of $1.4 million versus $600,000 for Tesco's.

So, in this e-commerce-enabled and highly disrupted world, supply chain improvement and innovation are the key to gaining a competitive advantage, as is discussed throughout this book [Hanks, 2013].

As has been discussed, to make omni-channel truly successful, you need to utilize demand shifting and shaping strategies, unified inventory and order views, and omni-channel network design. Technology is an important enabler in implementing these strategies, which we will discuss in our next chapter.

16

Technology as an Enabler of an Omni-Channel Retail Supply Chain

The supply chain operates with a variety of strategic, tactical, and operational systems, such as network optimization, demand forecasting, inventory management, warehouse, transportation, and reverse logistics management systems, which must be integrated on the back end for efficient supply chain management. In the case of omni-channel retail, they must also be integrated **on the front end** to ensure a seamless customer experience, as connecting technologies, e-commerce platforms, and other systems is essential.

SUPPLY CHAIN MACRO PROCESSES

Before delving into technology that can help enable omni-channel, we need to first understand some general components of supply chain technology. One way to look at the supply chain and its functional technology needs, at least at a high level, is by breaking it into macro processes. They are:

1. Supplier management (SM) – This macro process ensures that supplies are at the best cost and terms. It can include a strategic buy, a tactical negotiated purchase, or a heavily engineered item.
2. Internal supply chain management (ISCM) – Includes a number of activities with respect to the receiving, conversion, and movement of finished goods.

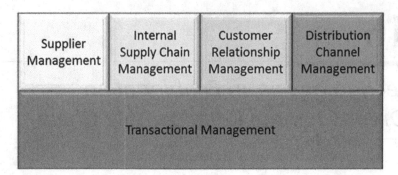

FIGURE 16.1
Supply chain macro processes.

3. Distribution channel management (DCM) – This macro process includes the links in a distribution network that has multi-tier arrangements. Specific processes depend upon the industry and type of products shipped and can also include service providers such as transportation, distribution, and third-party logistics (3PL) companies.

4. Customer relationship management (CRM) – Practices, strategies, and technologies that companies use to manage and analyze customer interactions and data throughout the customer lifecycle, with the goal of improving business relationships with customers, assisting in customer retention, and driving sales growth.

5. Transactional management (TM) – This entails the base transactional data such as order and inventory information to run the "day-to-day" aspects of a business.

Processes 1–4 above (as seen in Figure 16.1) provide access to and reporting of supply chain transaction data. Advanced systems use analytics based upon transaction data to improve supply chain performance, and enterprise resource planning (ERP) systems form the foundation of a supply chain IT system.

SUPPLY CHAIN INFORMATION TECHNOLOGIES

On a more practical level, supply chain management (SCM) systems can be also viewed in terms of planning (SCP) and execution (SCE) technologies tied to processes across the supply chain.

SCP applies algorithms to predict future requirements of various kinds and to help to balance supply and demand, and can include systems for demand management, supply management, and sales and operational planning (S&OP) to ensure supply matches demand.

Supply Chain Planning (SCP) Software

SCP software vendors address short- to long-term planning and focus on demand, supply, and the balance of demand and supply together, usually in the form of an S&OP process described in more detail below.

Demand management – There are three main functions of demand management software: (1) predicting demand, (2) using "what-if" analysis to create sales plans, and (3) using "what-if" analysis to shape demand. Forecasts are typically of a rolling 24–36 months. Modern supply chain systems have moved towards a demand "pull"-driven model so, as a result, demand management has moved from a purely forecasting tool to one that optimizes and shapes demand to some extent.

Supply management – This area helps meet demand with minimal resources at the lowest cost. Software functionality typically found in this area includes supply network planning or optimization (SNP), production scheduling (sometimes referred to as advanced planning systems (APS)), distribution requirements planning (DRP), replenishment, and procurement.

Sales and operational planning (S&OP) – Facilitates monthly executive planning meetings to tie together sales, operation, and financial plans, along with the related tasks, in an effort to make sure supply adequately meets demand at the lowest cost. Input is collected from demand, capacity, and financial plans, culminating in a consolidated sales and operational plan.

Supply Chain Execution (SCE) Software

SCE monitors the physical movement and status of goods as well as the management of materials and financial information of all participants in the supply chain, and can include systems such as warehouse management systems (WMS), transportation management systems (TMS), and enterprise resource systems (ERP), and feature planning, scheduling, optimizing, tracking, and performance monitoring as described below.

Warehouse management systems – WMS controls the flow of goods through the warehouse and interfaces with the material handling equipment. It also typically includes the automated processing of inbound and outbound shipments and the storage of goods. Administrative features can include the processing of EDI transactions, planning shipments, resource management, and performance tracking.

Transportation management systems – A TMS helps to manage global transportation needs including air, sea, ground, and carrier shipments. In terms of transportation acquisition and dispatching, a TMS may also handle the planning, scheduling, and optimizing of shipments. They also provide tracking of vehicles including exception management, constraints, collaborating with partners, and monitoring of freight. Administrative features can include cost allocations, freight auditing, and payment and contract management.

Enterprise resource systems (ERP) – While some may not include ERP systems as SCM tools, a great deal of the functionality is supply chain and logistics related. ERP systems are an extension of an MRP system tying in all internal processes as well as customers and suppliers. They allow for the automation and integration of many business processes including finance, accounting, human resources, sales and order entry, raw materials, inventory, purchasing, production scheduling, and shipping, resource and production planning, and customer relationship management. An ERP shares common databases and business practices and produces information in real time, and coordinates business from supplier evaluation to customer invoicing.

E-businesses must also keep track of and process a tremendous amount of information and, as such, have realized that much of the information they need to run an e-business such as stock levels at various warehouses, cost of parts, and projected shipping dates can already be found in their ERP system databases. As a result, a significant part of the online efforts of many e-businesses involves adding Web access to an existing ERP system.

ERP systems have the potential to reduce transaction costs and increase the speed and accuracy of information but can also be expensive and time-consuming to install.

Other Supply Chain Software Applications

There are also information technologies for:

Supply chain event management – Systems used for managing events that occur within and between organizations or supply chain partners. The goal is to keep all the users in the supply chain, from materials suppliers and buyers to warehouse managers and product carriers, informed about activity across the supply chain. They typically perform event monitoring, notification, simulation, control, and measurement processes.

Business intelligence (BI)/supply chain analytics – Applications, infrastructure, tools, and best practices to help turn data into actionable information through analysis to improve and optimize decisions and performance. These systems can include reports, real-time dashboards, and benchmarking.

Additionally, there are related tools for supply chain collaboration, data synchronization, and spreadsheets and database software.

While the types of software applications in supply chain probably won't drastically change, the methods for gathering data, and using and sharing applications will.

HARDWARE AND SOFTWARE TECHNOLOGY EXAMPLES

As information links all parts of the supply chain, there are other innovative hardware and software tool categories which help in this effort, in addition to the SCP and SCE technology mentioned above, such as:

Internet – Allows companies to communicate with suppliers, customers, shippers, and other businesses around the world, instantaneously.

E-business – Gradual replacement of physical business processes with electronic ones. Comes in two general forms, the largest being business-to-business (B2B), and the other being business-to-consumer (B2C).

Cloud-based hardware and software – Have enabled much of the information sharing that has accelerated supply chain flow, making comprehensive supply chain solutions affordable for even the smallest manufacturer, distributor, or retailer.

Mobile computing – Supply chain execution and event management is becoming more mobile with basic visibility and traceability available on smartphones and other mobile devices.

Third-party logistics (3PLs) companies providing technology – Cost is a big driver of this, as 3PLs can offer economies of scale, especially for small and mid-size companies.

Electronic data interchange (EDI) – The computer-to-computer exchange of standardized business documents. Today, EDI may also occur through the Internet.

Bar code and point-of-sale data – Creates an instantaneous computer record of a sale.

Radio-frequency identification (RFID) – Technology that can send product data from an item (containing an RFID chip) to a reader via radio waves. An RFID chip can be implemented in a variety of forms (e.g. a label or imbedded in between the cardboard layers in a carton or product packaging).

Internet of things (IoT) – The interconnection via the Internet of computing devices embedded in everyday objects, enabling them to send and receive data.

Artificial intelligence (AI), advanced robotics, and autonomous vehicles – There is a new generation of advanced robots and automated vehicles to track, locate, and move inventory within warehouses with enhanced sensing capabilities and AI algorithms, allowing them to better sense their environment and make decisions based on changes in that environment.

    While totally autonomous vehicles such as driverless trucks might not happen for a while, we are already seeing technology such as assisted braking, lane-assist, and highway autopilot, not to mention the use of drones (air and land) to deliver products to the customer.

OMNI-CHANNEL TECHNOLOGY TRENDS

While multi-channel retail is now the norm, as many retailers find it hard to have active presences on numerous channels and facilitate effective order fulfillment, integration across **all** the various channels, including social media, websites, brick-and-mortar stores, and marketplaces, is required to create the seamless omni-channel customer experience.

Areas where technology can help make this happen are:

- Technology has powered transparency, with increased visibility of operations and companies, as they have gone from being a black box to more of a glass box; those outside the box now have the ability to see the people, processes, and values. Consumers are concerned with fair labor practices, sustainable resourcing, and respect for a diversity of cultures. With easy access to social media forums, blogs, and other sites, consumers now have clarity and an understanding of how companies operate.
- Most major retailers today have an online presence and usually compete with one another on pricing, but what tends to differentiate these brands in the minds of consumers is often shipping. Supply chain technology industry disruptors, such as ShipBob, which through a network of fulfillment centers offers two-day shipping, are pushing the envelope.
- Immersive technologies including virtual reality (VR), augmented reality (AR), and mixed reality (MR) show consumers digital representations of how products would look in the home or on a person and can also be used to provide support for employee training and to increase the efficiency of warehouse operations. Consumers want interaction whether on mobile devices or social media, in retail stores, and through other channels so they can stay connected to the retailer throughout the entire sales journey.
- Consumers want retailers to personalize their service. Retailers collect, analyze, and consolidate data from an array of consumer channels which help them to better understand the motivation and preferences driving purchases so that they can design the needed touchpoints to connect buyers to the omni-channel retail journey. The goal, known as "omni-channel 2.0", is to streamline technology further to improve customer service, personalize the shopping experience, and create a more unified enterprise rather than just integrating legacy systems [datexcorp.com, 2019].

MOVING ON TO OMNI-CHANNEL 2.0

Traditional omni-channel refers to the blending of supply chain channels to allow customers to shop from any channel seamlessly, requiring supply chains to integrate storefronts, distribution centers, and online ordering processes into a single platform.

However, the reality is that many retailers have continued to use legacy systems through custom interfaces that lead to inefficiencies and integration problems.

Omni-channel 2.0, as mentioned in Chapter 14, is about bringing the entire enterprise together, not just enabling support within legacy systems, for an omni-channel approach to increase efficiency and transparency across all channels, engaging with consumers and personalizing the shopping experience.

To recap, the benefits of omni-channel 2.0 include:

- Greater control over key performance indicators.
- Flexible fulfillment options across multiple channels.
- End-to-end visibility.
- Better risk management strategies.
- Improved inventory management, reducing instances of overstocking and understocking.
- Improved IT processes and true integration between systems.

Not pursuing an omni-channel 2.0 strategy using enabling technology risks losing competitive advantage, higher overhead, and higher employee turnover rates.

Also, to summarize what was stated in Chapter 14, to utilize omni-channel 2.0, retailers need to:

- Integrate and widen their vendor base, allowing them to leverage the value of newer, more adaptable, and flexible supply chain systems.
- Focus on implementing omni-channel 2.0 with small changes, rather than one giant leap, to avoid disruptions.
- Develop a customer-centric strategy as it is difficult to meet omni-channel demand profitably (especially with legacy systems), so any investments in omni-channel should focus on improving profitability while meeting growing customer demands.
- Engage with customers for feedback in the development of omni-channel 2.0 to find out what you can do better to provide a superior customer experience.

All of this requires warehouses to move away from their legacy systems into the digital age with integrated, comprehensive platforms as customers want their products now, from any ordering portal, with the ability to pick up online orders from in-store (and other) locations, possibly having another item shipped to their home, while still having the option of getting notifications on their phones when they enter a store about items on sale [Rosing, 2019].

BEST PRACTICES TO LEVERAGE TECHNOLOGY

As you move from omni-channel 1.0 to 2.0, here are some best practices to help leverage technology to transform your supply chain processes, and improve costs and efficiencies:

Leverage big data – Buying patterns and customer behavior create challenges in managing inventory, so using software that can sense demand changes and help you react quickly to address supply constraints, optimize inventory, and improve in-stock performance is critical, not to mention the ability to streamline shipping and logistics services using dynamic routing (i.e. to determine the optimal delivery route). For example, Amazon uses big data to anticipate shipments by adjusting inventory before a customer places an order, using previous purchases.

Use master data platforms – Omni-channel means expanding beyond physical stores to online platforms and kiosks, so a consolidated platform using global master data management can deliver predictive analytics solutions to help you understand your customers better. It also allows you to increase efficiencies and security by centralizing data.

Conduct order fulfillment analysis – Logistics services use analytical tools in areas such as warehouse management to manage inventory levels as well as having analytical tools to optimize inventory at each stage of the supply chain and develop replenishment strategies. For example, Macy's realized that 15–20 percent of its inventory costs were associated with the last units of items in its stores as they were difficult to track. To improve accuracy, it now uses RFID technology to track last units and enhance order fulfillment, helping it to reduce $1 billion of inventory in its stores.

Ensure effective management of drop-ship vendors – Integrating drop-ship vendors into an order management system enables better communication and effective tracking of orders (the use of which is increasing substantially in an omni-channel environment). For example, Kroger collaborates with its vendors using a supply chain platform, sharing point of sale (POS) and inventory data with them, enabling them to work together as one team with a common view of inventory and customer activities.

Develop an omni-channel POS system – With the rising usage of mobile devices and increasing number of payment methods, it may be time to look at "state of the art" POS platforms. Omni-channel POS systems enable a uniform experience across e-commerce and brick-and-mortar stores and simplify transactions like "buy online pickup in store" (BOPIS) and "buy online return in store" (BORIS) by integrating transactions, including purchases, order reservations, in-store pickup, and online shipping.

Create a responsive omni-channel supply chain for higher business value – Today, most everyone recognizes the need to revamp their supply chain to be a successful omni-channel retailer. According to a Forrester survey on retailers in North America, 21 percent felt that omni-channel efforts were one of their leading priorities. Shoppers today want the best quality, costs, fulfillment time, and overall experience which is only possible with an agile and responsive supply chain that supports an omni-channel environment. Integrated front and back end systems, automation, and predictive analytics can help to achieve this requirement [Rikhy, 2016].

No one knows exactly how things will evolve in this omni-channel world, but we do know that there will be barriers to these potential changes with inherent risks. Let's now look at some of them as well as ways to mitigate risks.

Part V

The Shape of Things to Come

17

Barriers to Change and Mitigating Risk

As was stated early in this book, multi-channel retail is typically based on the assumption that customers choose a main way to connect, whether in physical stores or on a website on the Internet. While in an omni-channel environment, consumers are likely to have multiple touchpoints with a retailer and expect their interactions between each channel to be seamless. The idea is that a customer can order what they want, when they want, on whatever device they want, and have it delivered how they want (Figure 17.1).

It can be very hard to go from multi- to omni-channel as many surveys have found that very few retailers refer to themselves as fully omni-channel,

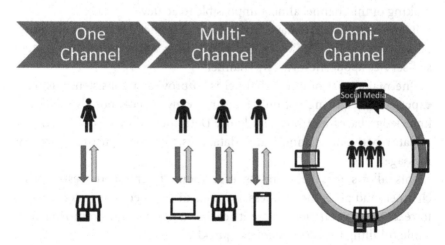

FIGURE 17.1
Omni-channel vs. multi-channel retail strategy.

with the majority (67 percent in an Evolve IP survey) stating that they are multi-channel. Obviously, the industry has a long way to go.

MAIN BARRIERS TO OMNI-CHANNEL

Three main barriers to omni-channel can be identified. They are:

1. Business processes are siloed.
2. The technology platform does not support a single view of the customer.
3. There is an insufficient budget to carry out the required changes.

The first step, as mentioned in the previous chapter, is to have a single integrated platform that can identify a customer regardless of the channel that they choose to use. To accomplish this will mean evolving from the siloed, channel-focused point solutions that were put in place to handle specific needs and using a services architecture that is extendable to different channels in the future.

Many businesses don't update customer records with details of non-voice interactions such as Web chat, letters, or social media interactions, making omni-channel almost impossible to achieve.

It is also important to have product and customer data as a single source of information that can be viewed in real time by the customer, agent, or self-service application via any channel.

One major goal of omni-channel is to provide a consistent customer experience, requiring not only the same view of data, but also the same knowledge bases and business logic. Data must flow in real time with updates between channels and databases, for the consistency of the message.

This allows for the seamless escalation of service requests within channels and gives the business a chance to use their automated systems to react to an escalation before it reaches a live agent, minimizing costs while fulfilling the service request quickly.

For example, an analysis of past interactions may show that a repeat customer is likely to reach out to the contact center within two days to check on its progress. Knowing this, the system can pre-empt this call before it reaches an agent, with the option to "check your order status" to reduce customer effort as well as the time and cost of the agent who would normally need to handle this.

As many businesses currently lack the necessary framework, resources, and capabilities to achieve omni-channel retail within their existing systems, they will need to completely overhaul their current systems and processes.

The cost of new systems, training, and achieving a single view of inventory can add up to a big initial investment for retailers, creating a significant barrier.

This risk can be offset by realizing the additional efficiencies of omni-channel retail along with many competitors moving in that direction as well. However, careful planning and selection of partners and systems are critical to avoid wasting time and money.

One emerging trend in omni-channel retail is "customer engagement hubs/centers" (CECs), which are a logical set of technologies and business applications that are engineered to provide customer service and support, regardless of the interaction (or engagement) channel including social media and community forums. The goal of CECs is to not only provide service to customers as they move among communications channels, but also to deliver the correct business rule determining the next best action, information, or process needed to engage the customers.

The CEC concept allows businesses to leave their CRM and multi-channel contact applications and infrastructure alone while being able to update and view an individual's customer record at any point in the customer journey [EvolveIP.com, 2018].

OTHER BARRIERS TO OMNI-CHANNEL

Some other barriers to omni-channel worth mentioning include:

Separate stock inventories prevent omni-channel retail – Omni-channel retail requires one single view of stock across the entire business, whether customers buy from a physical store, a website, a catalogue, or on mobile platforms. This allows for the proper placement of inventory for a seamless experience for customers, giving them a consistent service regardless of how they shop.

However, separate stock inventories are common and are a natural consequence of the dramatic growth of e-commerce, which causes big headaches for retailers as they try to provide a positive omni-channel customer experience. Without a single view, customers shopping online may be told that a product is no longer available, even if the item they want is sitting in a store somewhere. These separate stock inventories can result in more merchandise being bought, increasing the chances of future markdowns.

So, a single view of stock, besides enhancing the omni-channel experience, can also result in increased flexibility, a decreased need for end-of-season discounts, and less warehousing space required by retailers.

Different products, prices, and promotions across channels – Many retailers carry different products in each of their channels. Some items could be an online exclusive or only available in certain flagship stores. Promotions may also be applied to an item online, but not in store, and an increasing number of retailers offer online-only discount codes.

All of this can make ordering confusing for shoppers who may purchase an item in store, only to find out they could have paid less by ordering it from the same retailer online.

So, besides making omni-channel retail possible, a single set of products, prices, and promotions creates a seamless customer experience and makes marketing activities easier for businesses.

Inflexible partners make omni-channel retail impossible – Having inflexible and incompatible logistics partners can make omni-channel retail impossible to achieve, as omni-channel retail fulfillment can sometimes expose the inefficiency of the approach taken, negatively affecting the customer experience. So, it is extremely important to do proper vetting of potential logistics partners as to their omni-channel experience and expertise before entering into a long-term relationship [cmlplc.com, 2019].

BECOMING CUSTOMER- VS. CHANNEL-FOCUSED

Many retailers focus on individual "channels" within omni-channel and tend to treat each as a separate operation, neglecting the fact that shoppers will remain loyal only if retailers:

- Can deliver what they want, when and where they want it.
- Provide an experience, not just a product.
- Engage the consumer to build a relationship based on trust.

To stay relevant, retailers need to rethink how they attract and keep consumers. They should ask themselves: How are we set up to be able to quickly adapt and serve the consumer in the way that they expect? This new approach to business requires a culture shift. Those who are slow to pivot risk extinction.

IT STARTS WITH THE CONSUMER

Consumers' expectations are constantly evolving (look no further than the COVID-19 pandemic, where, at least in the short term, customers required curbside, no-contact pickups ordered online). Change happens on a daily basis, and the consumer (and the entire external environment) is driving it. But how do you rate the experience you're providing today? The right data and analytics can help.

Why limit analytics to reporting on sales, finance, supply chain, and investments, when there is a wide spectrum of data, internal and external, that can help you understand how you are actually serving your customers?

This type of analytics can tell you what customers are saying about your products and services on social networks as well as customer behavior in-store and online and the effectiveness of the characteristics you use to personalize product offerings.

Companies need to develop a good understanding of who their consumers are and to develop the ability to continue to learn as those consumers' tastes change.

LEAVE YOUR LEGACY (SYSTEMS AND PROCESSES) BEHIND

Many companies have a go-to-market approach that uses distinct channels, each with different goals and objectives. So, while in theory, they may be attempting to implement some kind of omni-channel approach, it will never be fully successful.

Their operations remain siloed in a number of ways, including:

- Inventory – Segmented by channel (i.e. wholesale, brick-and-mortar, and e-commerce).
- Fulfillment – Many use separate distribution channels and capabilities, including outsourcing, depending on where orders originate and need to be fulfilled from.
- Procurement and sourcing – Many businesses use different buyers and merchants for each channel.
- Finance and accounting – It's fairly common that many businesses don't have a method for allocating revenue for transactions with multiple touchpoints.

Due to resistance to change, instead of being able to capitalize on new ideas and innovation, omni-channel (and other) opportunities can get caught up in lengthy funding, approval, and resourcing processes.

As the COVID-19 pandemic has taught us, companies need to create a culture of change and flexibility, as the organization must be agile enough to pivot and meet changing needs quickly.

RETHINK YOUR BUSINESS

In this rapidly changing environment, companies need to rethink their total business. Some good places to start are the:

- Organization – Consider moving away from channel-specific titles, focusing your organization on the consumer and not your infrastructure, and give the executive in charge authority to make the necessary changes.
- Culture and governance – Create a culture focused on the consumer, establishing a set of processes that enable rapid decision-making and allocation of resources to meet consumer needs.

- Supply chain and operations – Source for all channels, have a single real-time view of your inventory, and demand and create an integrated fulfillment capability.

Create a technological platform that serves consumers as they want to be served, in a way that allows you to constantly fine-tune things [Hogenson, 2018].

MANAGING CHANGE IN TURBULENT TIMES

We are now in a "white-water rapids" phase in terms of the global economy, requiring flexibility from the processes, technology, and people in the supply chain to navigate these rough waters.

Making the transition to a truly flexible and lean supply chain, especially during these turbulent times, involves changing the three elements necessary for successful business transformation: Processes, technology, and people.

The transition involves using a structured approach to make sure that changes – which can range from a simple process tweak to major policy or strategy revisions – are implemented successfully if the organization is to achieve its potential.

REVISING PROCESSES

Companies can utilize many tools to manage process change in a supply chain. These tools include:

- **Benchmarking** to clearly identify performance gaps, and thus focus supply chain management efforts on the areas most in need of improvement.
- **Six Sigma** (often combined with lean) to improve quality throughout the supply chain.

- **Lean strategies** to streamline processes or eliminate waste within the supply chain.

TRANSFORMING TECHNOLOGY

Many companies are using digital technology to transform key business areas, but technology can't be applied haphazardly. When applied properly, however, it can enable good processes.

As discussed in the previous chapter, technological advancements have made it extremely easy to gather and analyze vast amounts of data. Focusing on key pieces of data used in decision-making saves time and money.

Many leading companies have gone further and have begun to create a true digital organization that automates repeatable tasks to increase efficiency and drive down costs.

MANAGING PEOPLE AND CHANGE

Few people like change within their organization, but if management leads the change initiative properly, the process can be successfully implemented with minimal resistance.

To effectively manage change in your organization, you must first educate leaders and gain their commitment and support for the effort. Leaders must communicate why the change is needed and what benefits they expect.

Leaders need to know when change is needed, work on getting the change accepted organizationally, implement change in the best way possible, and relate the need for change directly to the business value proposition.

For example, leadership needs to be able to clearly describe how improved demand planning helps sustain and increase revenues through improved customer satisfaction and reduced production, distribution, and inventory costs.

At this point, it is also important to identify risks and have a mitigation plan in place if issues arise. For example, consider piloting change in one location or business unit before rolling it out across the entire organization.

Furthermore, clearly defining roles and responsibilities within the organization will help earn employee buy-in and minimize confusion.

Finally, organizations must implement and continuously measure metrics – and design rewards – that reinforce and eventually maintain the desired future state.

In the end, creating a lean, flexible supply chain requires changes in your organization. It's up to you whether to cling to the past with the inherent risks or embrace change and look to the future [Myerson, 2019b].

MANAGING AND MITIGATING RISK

While the move to omni-channel retail can be difficult to accomplish as discussed above, it is also fraught with risks. If you're not prepared to deal with them in advance, it can have huge negative impacts on your business, as we've seen during the COVID-19 pandemic.

RIDING OUT THE (WHITE-WATER) RAPIDS

These days, it seems that we are moving from crisis to crisis – tariffs, a plummeting stock market, cyber-attacks, recalls, and the COVID-19 pandemic – at an ever-increasing pace. While we can't avoid these crises, we can minimize their impact with a lean, agile supply chain.

While that's easy to say, it's hard to do. Some key components to focus on include:

Supply chain visibility, both downstream and upstream – Better information sharing and collaboration with business partners and customers, along with a strong use of analytics, can help you anticipate and minimize the impact of disruptions.

Supply chain network optimization – Reduce network complexities and improve responsiveness to customer needs by optimizing asset locations across the supply chain. Develop an ongoing capability to evaluate business and environmental changes that affect the supply chain to increase flexibility while reducing costs and improving customer service.

Identify and mitigate risk – Global supply chains face increased risks from demand and supply variability, limited capacity, and quality issues. Identify the sources and types of potential risk and estimate their probability and impact. Then create and implement risk mitigation plans to minimize their impact.

Strategic sourcing formalizes the way organizations gather and use information to leverage consolidated purchasing power and find the best values in the marketplace. Sourcing strategies include outsourcing, insourcing, nearsourcing, few or many suppliers, and vertical integration.

INSTEAD OF A CRYSTAL BALL...

While it's difficult to predict the future, you can find help in a variety of ways.

Big data and predictive analytics can potentially provide insights that help you anticipate or respond to events or disruptions.

Cloud technology and the Internet of things (IoT) are expected to remove physical boundaries and create a centralized system, thereby increasing supply chain efficiency and productivity.

Next-gen analytics and artificial intelligence (AI) provide real-time, accurate information and insights that enable enterprises to rapidly adapt to shifts in the business landscape. AI-based technology helps supply chain professionals to strategize by providing insights and recommendations based on the study of market trends and automated forecasts.

So how do we manage our supply chain during these turbulent times? Consider these metaphors that describe how managers navigate change.

The "calm waters" metaphor is a description of traditional practices and theories that likens the organization to a large ship making a predictable trip across a calm sea and experiencing an occasional storm.

The "white-water rapids" metaphor describes the organization as a small raft navigating a raging river.

We are currently in a "white-water rapids" phase in terms of today's global economy, at least for the foreseeable future. So, it's best to strap on your safety belt and find ways to ride out these rapids, as supply chain risks have grown exponentially as we have moved to a global economy over the past 30 years [Myerson, 2019a].

So, let's first look at the history a bit before discussing the types of risks and how to mitigate them.

GROWTH OF GLOBALIZATION

In recent years, we have seen a change in how firms organize their production into global supply chains where companies are increasingly outsourcing some of their activities to third parties and are locating parts of their supply chain outside their home country (known as "offshoring").

They are also increasingly partnering with other firms through strategic alliances and joint ventures, enabling not only large but also smaller firms and suppliers to become global.

These types of global business strategies have allowed firms to specialize in "core" competencies to sustain their competitive advantage.

This is not limited to just outsourcing manufacturing and supply chain operations but also includes business process outsourcing (BPO) and information technology (IT) services, that are supplied from a large number of locations, as well as other knowledge-intensive activities such as R&D.

FACTORS INFLUENCING GLOBALIZATION

There are some key factors influencing the growth of globalization which has not just impacted manufacturing, but also retail, as many consumer products are sourced overseas. They include:

Improvements in transportation – Larger container ships mean that the cost of transporting goods between countries has decreased. Economies of scale are found as the cost per item can reduce when operating on a larger scale. Transportation improvements also mean that both goods and people can travel more quickly.

Freedom of trade – There are a number of organizations like the World Trade Organization (WTO) that promote free trade between countries, helping to remove barriers between countries.

Improvement of communications – The Internet and mobile technology have allowed greater communication between people in different countries.

Labor availability and skills – Less developed nations in Asia and elsewhere have lower labor costs and, in some cases, also high skill levels. Labor-intensive industries such as clothing can take advantage of cheaper labor costs and reduced legal restrictions in these less developed countries.

Transnational corporations – Globalization has resulted in many businesses setting up or buying operations in other countries. When a foreign company invests in a country, by building a factory or a shop, this is sometimes called inward investment. Companies that operate in several countries are often referred to as multinational corporations (MNCs) or transnational corporations (TNCs). The U.S. fast-food chain McDonald's is a large MNC, having nearly 30,000 restaurants in 119 countries.

Many multinational corporations not only invest in other economically developed countries, but also invest in less developed countries (e.g. Ford Motor Company makes large numbers of cars in the U.K. as well as in India).

REASONS FOR A COMPANY TO GLOBALIZE

The reasons a company may choose to globalize vary but are usually influenced by global, technological, cost, political, and economic influences. Some reasons to globalize within each of these influences include:

Global market forces

- Foreign competition in local markets.
- Growth in foreign demand.
- Global presence as a defensive tool.

- Companies forced to develop and enhance leading-edge technologies and products.

Technological forces

- Knowledge diffusion across national boundaries, hence the need for technology sharing to be competitive.
- Global location of R&D facilities.
- Close to production (as product cycles get shorter).
- Close to expertise (e.g. Indian programmers).

Global cost factors

- Availability of skilled or unskilled labor at lower cost.
- Integrated supplier infrastructure (as suppliers become more involved in design).
- Capital-intensive facilities utilize incentives such as tax breaks, price breaks, etc., which can influence the "make vs. buy" decision.

Political and economic factors

- Trade protection mechanisms such as tariffs, quotas, voluntary export restrictions, local content requirements, environmental regulations, and government procurement policies (discount for local).
- Customs duties which differ by commodity and the level of assembly.
- Exchange rate fluctuations and operating flexibility.

GLOBAL SUPPLY CHAIN STRATEGY DEVELOPMENT

Today, in most industries, it is necessary to develop a global view of your organization's operations to survive and thrive. However, many companies find it difficult to make the transition from domestic to international operations despite the fact that there have been significant improvements in transportation and technology over the past 25 years.

To be successful in the global economy, a company must have a supply chain strategy. This should include significant investments in ERP and other supply chain technology to prepare them to optimize global operations by linking systems across their business globally, helping them to better manage their global supply chains.

Earlier in this book we discussed omni-channel retail strategies and how the supply chain must support them. It is no different when discussing a global supply chain. In general, an organization should have their global supply chain set up to maximize customer service at the lowest possible cost.

Kauffman and Crimi, in their paper "A Best-Practice Approach for Development of Global Supply Chains" [Kauffman et al., 2005], suggest that developing a global supply chain not only requires the same information as when developing one domestically, but also requires additional information on international logistics, law, customs, culture, ethics, language, politics, government, and currency. Cross-functional teams should be utilized that are supplied with detailed information including the "what, when, and where" of the global supply chain as well as quantity demand forecasts. Supplier evaluations must examine their ability to handle international operations and subsequent requirements.

To actually implement a global supply chain for your business, after identifying your supply chain partners, the team should document and test the required processes and procedures before implementing. All participants must be trained in the processes and procedures, with metrics established to manage and control the global operations. The team must establish a project plan with responsibilities and milestones for the implementation.

The actual step-by-step approach for developing global supply chains recommended by Kauffman and Carmi is as follows:

1. Form a cross-functional global supply chain development team.
   - Include all affected parties, internal and external.
   - The team composition may change as development and implementation proceeds.
2. Identify needs and opportunities for supply chain globalization.
   - Determine the requirements your supply chain must meet.
     - Commodities, materials, services required ... dollar value of materials and services ... importance of commodities, materials, and services...
     - Performance metrics for qualification and evaluation of suppliers.
   - Determine the current status of your supply chain "as is".

- Existing suppliers of materials and services.
- Customers...
- Commodity markets...
- Current performance, problem areas.
- Competitiveness...
- "Fit" of your current supply chain with your operational requirements.

The main components of this particular framework ... should include all operational dimensions of supply chains which must be identified, considered, and included in any determination of requirements and assessment of current status of supply chains.

3. Determine commodity/service priorities for globalization consideration based on needs and opportunities.
4. Identify potential markets and suppliers and compare to "as is" markets, suppliers, and supply chain arrangements, operations, and results.
5. Evaluate/qualify markets and suppliers, identify supplier pool (determine best ones based on likely total cost of ownership (TCO), and best potential to meet or exceed expectations and requirements).
6. Determine selection process for suppliers, e.g. request for proposal (RFP), negotiation, etc.
7. Select suppliers or confirm current suppliers.
8. Formalize agreements with suppliers.
9. Implement agreements.
10. Monitor, evaluate, review and revise as needed [Kauffman et al., 2005].

GLOBAL SUPPLY CHAIN RISKS AND CHALLENGES

The global supply chain is fraught with risks and challenges.

As operations become more complex, logistics becomes more challenging, lead times lengthen, costs increase, and customer service can suffer. With a global footprint, different products are directed to more diverse customers via different distribution channels, requiring different supply chains.

There are many other, additional issues to address such as the identification of sources capable of producing the materials in the quality and quantity required, the protection of a firm's intellectual property, understanding import/export compliance issues, communication with suppliers and transportation companies, differences in time zones, language, and technology, and product security while in transit.

QUESTIONS TO CONSIDER WHEN GOING GLOBAL

All of this raises some initial questions that companies need to consider as their operations globalize, as was pointed out in a PWC-MIT forum on supply chain innovation [www.pwc.com, 2013].

The questions and findings from the forum were:

1. What are the drivers of supply chain complexity for a company with global operations?

   Supply chains are exposed to both domestic and international risks. The more complex the supply chain, the less predictable the likelihood and the impact of disruption. Over recent years, the size of the supply chain network has increased, dependencies between entities and between functions have shifted, the speed of change has accelerated, and the level of transparency has decreased.

   Overall, developing a product and getting it to the market require more complex supply chains, needing a higher degree of coordination.

2. What are the sources of supply chain risk?

   Risks to global supply chains vary from controllable to uncontrollable ones and include:
   - Raw material price fluctuation
   - Currency fluctuations
   - Market changes
   - Energy/fuel price volatility
   - Environmental catastrophes
   - Raw material scarcity
   - Rising labor costs
   - Geopolitical instability

3. What parameters are supply chain operations most sensitive to?

   Respondents replied that their supply chain operations were most sensitive to reliance on skill-set and expertise (31 percent), price of commodities (29 percent), and energy and oil (28 percent). For example, when U.S. diesel prices rose significantly in 2012, shippers rapidly adjusted budgets in order to offset the increased costs produced by higher fuel prices.

4. How do companies mitigate against disruptions?

A great majority of respondents (82 percent) said they had business continuity plans ready. Nissan, for example, had a well-thought-out and exercised business continuity plan ready to kick into action to facilitate a quick recovery. Other major strategies of respondents included:

- Implement dual sourcing strategy.
- Use both regional and global strategy.
- Pursue (first- and second-tier) supplier collaboration.
- Pursue demand collaboration with customers.

KEY GLOBAL SUPPLY CHAIN CHALLENGES

According to a survey by PRTM consultants for Supply Chain Digest [www.scdigest.com, 2010], key global supply chain challenges include:

Supply chain volatility and uncertainty have permanently increased – Market transparency and greater price sensitivity have led to lower customer loyalty. Product commoditization reduces true differentiation in both the consumer and business-to-business (b2b) environments...

Securing growth requires truly global customer and supplier networks – Future market growth depends on international customers and customized products. Increased supply chain globalization and complexity need to be managed effectively...

Market dynamics demand regional, cost-optimized supply chain configurations – Customer requirements and competitors necessitate regionally tailored supply chains and product offerings. End-to-end supply chain cost optimization will be critical...

Risk management involves the end-to-end supply chain – Risk and opportunity management should span the entire supply chain—from demand planning to expansion of manufacturing capacity—and should include the supply chains of key partners...

Existing supply chain organizations are not truly integrated and empowered – The supply chain organization needs to be treated as a single integrated organization. In order to be effective, significant improvements require support across all supply chain functions.

RISK MANAGEMENT

An organization's supply chain is greatly impacted by globalization and its inherent logistical complexity. This has resulted in having risk beyond just the demand and supply variability, limited capacity, and quality issues that domestic companies have traditionally faced, to now include other trends such as greater customer expectations, global competition, longer and more complex supply chains, increased product variety with shorter lifecycles, security, and political and currency risks.

As a result, it is important for global supply chain managers to be aware of the relevant risk factors and build in suitable mitigation strategies.

Potential Risk Identification and Impact

Before planning for risks in your supply chain, you must first identify potential risks as well as their impact.

To accomplish this, many companies use a "vulnerability map" or risk-matrix to visualize unforeseen and unwanted events as shown in Figure 17.2 [Sheffield and Rice, Jr., 2005].

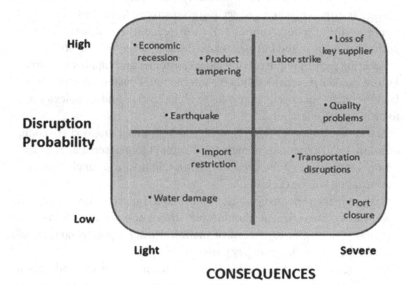

FIGURE 17.2
"Vulnerability map."

This type of analysis has two dimensions: Disruption probability and consequences. Obviously, risks with a high disruption probability and severe consequences should be given a great deal of attention.

One problem with this method is that it relies heavily on risk perception, which can vary depending on recent events, a person's experience and knowledge, their appetite for risk, and their position in the organization, among other things.

Sources of Risk

Before determining a risk management strategy for your organization, it is important to consider the possible sources of risk. There are five sources of risk in a supply chain, some of which are internal, others external to your organization [Figure 17.3; Christopher and Peck, 2004].

Internal Risks

Process risk refers to the value-adding and managerial activities undertaken by the firm and to disruptions to these processes. These processes are usually dependent on internally owned or managed assets and on the existing infrastructure, so the reliability of supporting transportation, communication, and infrastructure should be carefully considered.

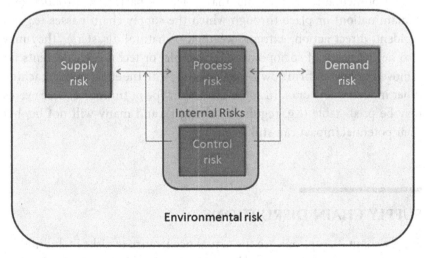

FIGURE 17.3
Sources of risk in the supply chain.

Control risks are the rules, systems, and procedures that determine how organizations exert control over the processes and are therefore the risks arising from the use (or mis-use) of these rules. For the supply chain, they include order quantities, batch sizes, safety stock policies, etc., and any policies and procedures that cover asset and transportation management.

External Risks

Demand and supply risks are external to the organization, but are internal to the networks through which materials, products, and information flow between companies. The organization should consider potential disruptions to the flow of product and information from within and between all parties in the extended supply chain network and at least understand and monitor the potential risks that may affect other supply chain partners.

Supply risk is the upstream equivalent of demand risk and relates to potential or actual disturbances to the flow of product or information from within the network, upstream of your organization (COVID-19 is a current example).

Environmental risks are disruptions that are external to the network of organizations through which the products flow. This type of event can impact your organization directly, those upstream or downstream, or the marketplace itself.

Environmental-related events may affect a particular product (e.g. contamination) or place through which the supply chain passes (e.g. an accident, direct action, extreme weather, or natural disasters). They may also be the result of sociopolitical, economic, or technological events far removed from your firm's own supply chains, with the effects often reaching other industry networks. In some cases, the type or timing of these events may be predictable (e.g. regulatory changes), and many will not be, but their potential impact can still be evaluated.

SUPPLY CHAIN DISRUPTIONS

Supply chain disruptions are the actual occurrence of risks including the categories mentioned above and are unplanned and unanticipated events that disrupt the normal flow of goods and materials within a supply chain.

There is usually some triggering event followed by the situation (with its consequences) that occurs afterwards.

Disruptions that a company has to deal with come primarily, although not always as previously mentioned, from customers, suppliers, and/or the supply chain. The consequences can be immense for your company and can include higher costs, poor performance, lost sales, lower profits, bankruptcy, and damage to your organization.

The actual characteristics of the supply chain structure you have may determine the drivers of your supply chain's vulnerability.

These characteristics may include:

- Complexity of the supply chain (e.g. global vs. domestic sourcing).
- Density of the supply chain (i.e. using these high-density regions leads to higher vulnerability of supply chains).
- Single or sole sourcing vs. multiple vendors for the same item.
- Lean and JIT production philosophies require precise timing.
- The centralization of warehouse/manufacturing locations results in lengthy lead times due to distance issues.
- Dependency on major suppliers/customers (i.e. the "all your eggs in one basket" syndrome).
- Dependency on IT infrastructure, electricity, etc.

Flexible, secure supply chains with a diversified supplier base are less vulnerable to disruptions than those that are not.

Therefore, to a great degree, potential disruptions are the result of "conscious" decisions regarding how you design the supply chain. Risk management is about using innovative planning to reduce potential disruptions by preparing responses for negative events.

RISK MITIGATION

Depending on the type of supply chain risk, what follows are some common supply chain risks and tactics for risk mitigation [Heizer and Render, 2013]:

Supplier failure to deliver – Use multiple suppliers with contracts containing penalties. When possible, keep subcontractors on retainer.

Example: McDonald's planned its supply chain for many years before opening stores in Russia. All plants are monitored closely to ensure strong links.

Supplier quality failure – Ensure that you have adequate supplier selection, training, certification, and monitoring processes.

Example: Darden Restaurants (i.e. Olive Garden restaurants) has used third-party audits and other controls on supplier processes and logistics for the reduction of risk.

Logistics delays or damage – Have multiple or backup transportation modes and warehouses. Make sure that you have secure packaging and execute contracts with penalties for non-conformance.

Example: Walmart always plans for alternative origins and delivery routes, bypassing problem areas when delivering from its distribution centers to its stores with its private fleet.

Distribution – Have a detailed selection and management process when using public warehouses. Make sure that your contracts have penalties for non-conformance.

Example: Toyota trains its dealers on improving customer service, logistics, and repair facilities.

Information loss or distortion – Always back up databases within secure information systems. Use established industry standards and train supply chain partners on the understanding and use of information.

Example: Boeing utilizes a state-of-the-art international communication system that transmits engineering, scheduling, and logistics data to Boeing facilities and suppliers worldwide.

Political – Companies can purchase political risk insurance. This is also the situation where you may decide to go the route of franchising and licensing with your business.

Example: Hard Rock Cafe restaurants try to reduce political risk by franchising and licensing, in countries where they deem that the political and cultural barriers are great.

Economic – Hedging, the act of entering into a financial contract in order to protect against unexpected, expected, or anticipated changes in currency exchange rates, can be used to address exchange rate risk.

Example: Honda and Nissan have moved some of their manufacturing processes out of Japan since the exchange rate for the yen has made Japanese-made automobiles more expensive.

Natural catastrophes – In many cases, natural disasters can be planned for by taking out various forms of insurance (e.g. flood insurance). Companies may also consider alternate sourcing for example.

Example: Toyota, after the 2011 earthquake and tsunami, has established at least two suppliers, in different geographical regions, for each component.

Theft, vandalism, and terrorism – Again, in some cases, there is insurance available for these types of risk. Companies also enforce patent protection and use security measures such as RFID and GPS.

Example: Domestic Port Radiation Initiative: The U.S. government has established radiation monitors at all major U.S. ports that scan imported containers for radiation.

The Road Map out of This Mess

For years, I have been a proponent of operating a lean and agile supply chain, but some now say the COVID-19 pandemic has revealed the shortcomings of a supply chain that is perhaps too lean.

To be "lean", however, doesn't mean maintaining extremely low inventory levels with no coordination or backup plan. It also appears some have forgotten the "agile" part, meaning you need flexible alternatives at the ready.

In any case, it appears that many companies and their supply chains were caught off guard by the COVID-19 crisis despite recent disasters such as the earthquake and tsunami in Japan, volcanic eruptions in Iceland, and Hurricanes Maria and Harvey.

As stated earlier, in order to minimize risk in their supply chains, companies need to first identify the sources and types of potential risk and estimate their probability and impact. Supply chain risks come from an array of potential sources, including global pandemics.

Risk Mitigation Strategies

To combat this type of scenario, companies should look to supply chain risk mitigation strategies that include boosting capacity, engaging redundant suppliers, increasing responsiveness and flexibility, aggregating demand, and increasing source capabilities. Where appropriate, companies also can consider adding inventory by decentralizing the stock of predictable, lower-value products and centralizing the stock of less predictable, higher-value products (such as personal protective equipment and ventilators in our current case).

Where to Start

According to a 2015 Deloitte survey, while many company executives realized supply chain risk was an important factor in their decision-making, many didn't feel their programs were effective. I don't think things have changed much since then.

A good place to start in the risk mitigation process is by mapping your supply chain. Make sure you know the answer to questions such as:

- The physical locations of your suppliers' manufacturing facilities, and those of their suppliers.
- Which parts are manufactured at each location.
- The history and frequency of disruptions that occur at each facility and geographic region, due to either natural forces (hurricanes, floods, earthquakes) or other factors (labor strikes, power outages, quality issues).

Many sophisticated software tools are available to help map your supply chain. Smaller companies that can't afford the investment can analyze their bill of materials and focus on key components.

Work from the Top Down

This analysis typically starts with the top products by revenue, working down through their component suppliers and their suppliers, all the way to raw materials suppliers. The goal is to go down as many tiers as possible.

The map should also include information about which activities a primary site performs, alternate sites the supplier has that could perform the same activities, and the lead time for the supplier to begin shipping from the backup site.

Companies that invested in mapping their supply networks before the pandemic were better prepared with clearer visibility of the structure of their supply chains. The mapping gives them a vast resource of information at their fingertips within minutes of a potential disruption.

Mapping helps you determine which suppliers, sites, parts, and products are at risk, allowing your company priority to secure constrained inventory and capacity from suppliers at alternate sites [Myerson, 2020].

While this chapter focused on barriers and risks to change (in general and in the case of moving to omni-channel), it's time to look at the opposite end of the spectrum, the enablers of a true omni-channel experience for your customers.

18

Key Enablers of Omni-Channel

The growing need for a seamless, accurate, timely, and personalized omni-channel response is coming at us at an ever-increasing rate.

Consumer demands coupled along with trends such as shorter product lifecycles, free shipping, and competition around delivery times mean retailers can't operate within channel silos anymore. They need to anticipate and stay ahead of market disruptions such as COVID-19 and be agile and flexible enough to rapidly adapt to consumer expectations. The retailers who try to use legacy systems and processes to meet these new consumer demands may lose market share, and struggle to stay profitable.

To remain competitive, at the minimum they must:

- Meet customers in the channel of their choice.
- Recognize and acknowledge who individual customers are, the products and services they have purchased, and their prior interaction history, regardless of channel.
- Operate as a single brand and channel, orchestrating customer experiences across all touchpoints.
- Show customers they are valued through personalized offers, treatments, and rewards.

What are some concerns of retailers when it comes to successfully implementing an omni-channel strategy?

AREAS OF ATTENTION

"Omni-Channel Retail, A Deloitte Point of View" (2015) identified three areas that require attention during the shift towards omni-channel retail:

1) Return on marketing spend – As we know, omni-channel marketing is about delivering a more interactive, personalized brand experience that goes beyond siloed behavior, where the consumer is reached through all possible touchpoints or channels. Both e-tailers and traditional retailers need to create a marketing strategy specific to their business and products, with the marketing going through the appropriate channels for each customer group.

2) Ever-changing payment solution landscape – While multiple payment solutions have existed in the e-commerce market for some time, it is only recently that it has become a consideration for driving sales across the various channels. Online customers expect multiple payment options, requiring retailers to offer the right mix of payment options.

3) Increased supply chain complexity – The supply chain supports e-commerce operations as the organization and execution of the entire integrated supply chain will determine the customer experience. A supply chain with optimized and aligned warehousing and distribution operations can help you to deliver on your promises, as well as the management of returns, with its inherent high costs.

OMNI-CHANNEL SUPPLY CHAIN ENABLERS

Delving a little more into the supply chain area, which requires much attention (as that is the primary focus of this book), Deloitte found that customer-driven delivery and return strategies were critical enablers of an omni-channel strategy.

Specifically, the enablers mentioned included:

Drop-shipping – This is where a customer order triggers a shipment from a third-party logistics provider (3PL) or direct from the manufacturer, and can be an effective way for e-tailers to reduce inventory holding costs and warehouse space, freeing up capital for other investments.

Drop-shipping may not be applicable in all industry segments. For example, in fashion, customers may order multiple products from different brands, but would expect one delivery, not multiple shipments from different vendors. On the other hand, in the furniture industry, drop-shipping works quite well as it can lower margins since the 3PL or manufacturer builds inventory holding costs into the price.

Click-and-collect – This is where the customer purchases items online and has the option to pick up at a brick-and-mortar (or other designated) location of the customer's choosing. While it may seem easy, it is a challenging strategy to actually implement. However, click-and-collect does give customers flexibility and control over their purchase because they are able to choose a convenient location from which to pick up their item.

Curbside pickup (often "contactless") – A variation on click-and-collect, it is gaining popularity during the COVID-19 pandemic, and allows the customer to place their order online or by phone (typically requires payment upfront via credit card, PayPal, etc.) and to pick up curbside at the retail location later. While this began at restaurants and grocery stores, it has rapidly gained popularity in other types of retail. Only time will tell if this is a lasting option after the pandemic is behind us.

Reserve-and-collect – This is similar to click-and-collect, except that checkout occurs after the customer views the item(s) in person. The customer reserves an item online and picks it up and pays for it later at a brick-and-mortar store, requiring retailers to have very organized inventory supported by a good order management system.

Delivery lockers – Lockers are placed in convenient locations such as train stations and grocery stores. The customer opens the locker with a code given to them in connection with a purchase online. Customers can also return items to the lockers, but this can become an issue during periods of peak sales.

Same-day delivery – Customers are increasingly requiring fast delivery, so being able to provide same-day delivery can give your company a competitive advantage. From a fulfillment strategy standpoint, this means the item ordered is in stock in a brick-and-mortar store or a warehouse that is located close to a major city and is delivered on the same day to the customer. This type of delivery can be extremely challenging outside of larger cities and only works in some industries.

Many (Un)Happy Returns: Return Strategy as an Enabler

The high costs associated with returns (up to 40 percent in some industries) continues to challenge the e-commerce industry. Customers expect generous return policies, especially when buying in an omni-channel environment when they usually don't physically see and touch the product before buying it.

Customers also expect longer free return periods for products bought online as well as to be able to return an item wherever they like.

A generous return policy can drive sales (e.g. Zappos and Warby Parker), but it is also a major cost driver. Omni-channel retailers that can figure out how to combine a generous policy that drives additional sales, while optimizing the costs of returns management, will be the leaders of tomorrow. If properly handled, returns can largely contribute to increased revenues or, if not handled well, reduce profits through higher transportation, handling, and warehouse costs.

Technology as an Enabler

Dynamically changing supply chain and fulfillment strategies have increased the importance for an enterprise-wide system for inventory that breaks down barriers and integrates channels with each other to create the better visibility needed for an omni-channel experience.

A truly integrated order management system (OMS) is critical in omni-channel retail, since the customer interacts with and moves between physical and digital channels.

OMS is becoming increasingly important as it is at the center of e-commerce operations, integrating the order and delivery channels, not only processing orders, but also providing intelligence and visibility surrounding inventory, delivery options, and customer information.

It is important to have a good OMS to offer the various delivery options today's customer is demanding, as it has to share information about the order throughout the entire order cycle, from the point of order to the final delivery, and provide the organization with real-time information regardless of the delivery channel or point of order.

Benefits of an Omni-Channel OMS

Below are some of the benefits of an integrated OMS in an omni-channel environment:

- Distributed order management – An OMS assists with order routing, returns management, order splitting, tax calculations, payment processing, partial shipments, and order exception management, all critical components for e-tailers.
- Single view of inventory – As has been mentioned in numerous parts of this book, having a single view of inventory is critical to success in omni-channel retail and its supply chain, as it can provide real-time information about available inventory across all channels in the organization. An OMS can also combine an "outside in" view of inventory information with an "inside out" view, seamlessly integrating internal store and distribution inventory with drop-ship vendors, in-transit inventory, and third-party delivery facilities.
- Store fulfillment – The rising trend of store fulfillment is important for e-tailers that also have physical stores, as it provides information on shipping e-commerce orders from stores, store pickup, and click-and-collect.
- Customer service – Of course, OMS is an effective way to increase customer service as it provides information about order details, order capture, and refunds/credits, among other things.

NEXT STEPS IN YOUR SUPPLY CHAIN'S OMNI-CHANNEL JOURNEY

The question then becomes: "How can your organization take the next step in its omni-channel evolution?"

To do this, you need to know where you are and where you want to be. Table 18.1 is a great starting point. I am a firm believer in "evolution not revolution", so I wouldn't recommend skipping any steps.

TABLE 18.1

Supply Chain Omni-Channel Evolution

Entry-Level: Functionality Does Not Exist	Developing: Basic Functionality Exists	Performing: Advanced Functionality Exists	Leading: Industry Leader
No clear vision exists for e-commerce supply chain and order fulfillment	A supply chain strategy with a clear vision exists for the e-commerce operations	The supply chain strategy is well-designed and executed with the use of systems (WMS, OMS, etc.)	A tailored supply chain with a mix of fulfillment strategies
Limited shipping options offered to customers	Several shipping options, treated as separate/isolated channels, are available to the customers	Optimized returns management	Real-time tracking of order and shipment is made available to the customer
Shipments are made on an ad-hoc basis	Shipments are planned and consolidated where possible, with accurate estimated vs. actual delivery dates	Multiple shipping and delivery options exist (e.g. click-and-collect, same-day delivery, etc.) with integration between the various channels	Order fulfillment and shipments are enabled by technologies
No strategy for optimizing returns management	Policies are developed for returns management to reduce cost	Shipment and return KPIs are tracked and benchmarked against industry peers	Seamless integration between all channels

Source: "Omni-Channel Retail, A Deloitte Point of View", Deloitte, 2015.

Some organizations are just starting their omni-channel journey; others are already well on their way with varying degrees of success. No matter where you are in this journey, it's important to consider what tomorrow may bring us as we will discuss in the next and final chapter.

19

What Tomorrow May Bring Us

In the past year or so, you may have seen some headlines such as "Omni-Channel Is Dead", "The Death of Omni-Channel and the Emergence of Transact-Anywhere", "Omni-Channel Is Dead; Long Live Omni-Relationship", etc.

As Mark Twain said after his obituary had been mistakenly published, "reports of my death are greatly exaggerated".

The reality is that whatever you want to call it, omni-channel is here to stay. The question is, how will it evolve?

One big mistake retailers have made is to think too much in terms of channels and not enough about the customer and their experience. It should be a seamless experience moving from channel to channel; retailers should not focus on an individual channel, trying to make that experience the best. In essence, the customer is the channel (a "blended" channel at that).

A couple of examples of retailers who have achieved this concept of a "blended" channel are:

Crate & Barrel – The large home goods retailer realized that customers moved from mobile to tablet while doing research and purchasing, so they allowed for a "saving of shopping cart" option available in all channels to bring ease to the transition.

Oasis – A U.K. fashion retailer, Oasis realized that a major issue was the unavailability of stock at the e-commerce site and in retail stores. So they supplied retail associates with iPads to order online for customers in case the item is out of stock at a physical location, and, if an item is sold out online, customers can use Oasis' "Seek & Send" service that searches its stores for the product and ships it to the shopper.

Furthermore, it is becoming increasingly clear that to support the idea of focusing on the seamless customer experience, the different "touchpoints" shouldn't compete but be complementary [absolutdata.com, 2015].

To accomplish this, retailers also need to leverage customer insight (i.e. use data analytics) to understand how customer segments navigate the customer journey across digital and physical channels. By using this information, retailers can execute a seamless retail experience by eliminating the friction points.

WHATEVER WE CALL IT, IT'S HAPPENING

No matter what we call it, there are still many retailers who haven't moved away from siloed channels towards an "omni-channel" or "fill in the blank" (unified commerce, harmonized retail, transact-anywhere, etc.) approach. There is no question that it's happening whether retailers like it or not, but it is not easy.

As we have discussed, a unified, real-time view of inventory across the channels is critical for customers. Real-time inventory is not widely available today in many organizations, and legacy systems can't handle the routing necessary to make "ship from anywhere" an executable, cost-effective concept.

If you want to have product available when, where, and how the customer wants it, then inventory needs to be available in the network (including physical stores) to make this achievable. The product mix and inventory levels at stores need to be adjusted to allow for new functionality such as buy online, pick up in store.

Retailers can negate the impact of the in-store aspects of omni-channel (e.g. sold in store, but fulfilled elsewhere or vice-versa) by ensuring associates are both trained and incentivized to participate in cross-channel commerce, as well as making sure there is adequate space in the store for staging, packing, and shipping orders.

To summarize what's driving this change, Three Deep Marketing stated that while only 8 percent of retailers believe they have achieved a successful omni-channel strategy, an overwhelming 87 percent of retailers believe that an omni-channel strategy is critical to success. Furthermore, they found that companies with omni-channel customer engagement strategies keep an average of 89 percent of their customers as compared with a retention rate of only 33 percent for companies with weak omni-channel engagement [Three Deep Marketing, 2019].

WHAT DOES THE FUTURE HOLD FOR OMNI-CHANNEL RETAILING?

Some believe that customers are looking for deeper relationships with the brands they engage with and as a result will expect a shopping experience that gets them what they want, when they want it, quickly and efficiently, and if they can't find it from one brand, they will move on quickly.

If this is true, then omni-channel retail needs to be a top priority for retailers and needs to be implemented quickly to maintain a competitive advantage (as we are seeing during the COVID-19 pandemic).

Data Analytics and Artificial Intelligence (AI)

Omni-channel analytics can be defined as the use of data from multiple channels to improve all retail operations while also improving the customer experience. It's accomplished through a strong data strategy, analytical merchandising, intelligent marketing, and an open ecosystem for analytics.

Some of what retailers can accomplish with omni-channel analytics includes:

- Focus your marketing by understanding your customer better, knowing how digital and physical channels affect one another, building targeted marketing to cover the multitude of interactions and consumers each day.
- Optimize merchandizing by knowing which stores have similar product requirements, creating customer-centric assortments, and having a pricing strategy for each product lifecycle.
- Adjust your supply chain by determining if promotions work across channels to predict demand, have optimal levels of inventory, and fulfill e-commerce orders in the correct locations to minimize shipping costs.

- Improve store operations by analyzing your business, knowing what drives the customer purchases, communicating with customers in real time, and determining optimal staffing and product placement to improve productivity and increase sales.
- Improve cybersecurity by making your network secure, uncovering suspicious activities to protect customers, minimize fraudulent activities, and reduce losses [SAS Insights, 2020].

AI to Enhance the Omni-Channel Experience

As the omni-channel experience is about connecting the physical world and the digital experience, there is now a focus on context and using current technologies such as text-based support or even in-app support options to provide better digital experiences and customer service.

Here are some specific ways in which AI technologies will help improve omni-channel capabilities in a world of rising customer expectations:

1. Meet expectations and minimize the cost to serve – Retailers spend up to 18 percent of every revenue dollar generated online to meet customer expectations according to the JDA PWC annual retail CEO survey. Cognitive tools allow retailers to gather data on their cost to serve, to then understand different ways to increase their profits and meet customer expectations, such as choosing the right delivery path that prioritizes speed and minimizes delivery cost and other factors.
2. Maximize omni-channel fulfillment capacity – AI tools help create a strategy that's flexible enough to meet the customer's ever-varying buying journey. Real-time information makes it possible to move returns and existing inventory to meet increased demand and anticipate changes with scenario planning strategies to map out cost-efficient options to maximize customer service.
3. Use inventory at its most profitable price point – Not many retailers (10 percent in PWC survey) have refined their omni-channel delivery to the point that they can both meet demand and make a profit. A variety of issues including slow/non-moving inventory, returns, and markdowns play a role in cutting into profits. AI tools can help retailers to focus on using inventory to minimize carrying cost and limit markdowns and other promotions.

4. Make dynamic adjustments – Accessing real-time data helps retailers to take actions sooner without the need to open IT tickets or initiate cross-platform communications. Using real-time insights from AI tools, retail managers can see up-to-the-minute trends and demand so that they can take quick action.

Artificial intelligence can power the omni-channel and change how retailers market and provide an overall better experience for employees and customers.

As digital transformation evolves there should always be a continued focus on the customer experience. Connecting people to the right content at the right time across any device needs to be effortless, consistent, and contextual and will be the foundation for the evolution of digital transformation [Orchestra CMS, 2020].

Barriers for Growth of Omni-Channel

An omni-channel model that gives consumers the best features of traditional shopping combined with the advantages of e-commerce will be a key to the future of retail.

In a 2017 survey, the 60+ age group was open to online shopping for at least some products with, not surprisingly, younger age groups being much more open to the idea. Nevertheless, online sales still only account for 15 percent of the non-food market in much of North America and Europe, and just 3 percent in food in 2017.

Two factors have been blocking retailers' online businesses: The digital shopping experience and the costs of fulfillment and last-mile delivery.

There are some developments in both areas on the horizon which may lead to major advances...

Make It Fun, Make It Easy

While the online shopping experience improved significantly in the past 15 years, for many customers online browsing is not as intuitive as walking through a store, especially when assembling large, complicated shopping carts as customers do for groceries.

For customers who are less comfortable with the Web or mobile browsers, voice-recognition technology such as Amazon's Alexa or Google

Home may help. Other innovations such as augmented and virtual reality make the online experience more compelling (e.g. VR applications that let consumers experiment with different looks help sell make-up online).

The digital experience may even surpass physical stores by developing personalized curation services, such as those offered by Cladwell and Thread which provide customers advice they would get from the best stores, as they work with algorithms that know far more about the customer than shop assistants. The technology could be licensed to multiple retailers, saving them the development costs.

Last-Mile Delivery

Efficient fulfillment and last-mile operations are critical for all retailers, as the costs of picking and delivering online orders are quite large. Retailers typically either pass some of these costs onto the customer through fees or a large minimum order, or they take a profit hit from absorbing these (most companies end up shouldering 25 percent of the delivery cost). This can often mean they will offer fewer delivery slots to save costs. That is why reducing the cost of last-mile delivery is a key to improving this aspect of the consumer experience and increasing adoption and why companies like Amazon are experimenting with everything from drones to "Amazon Logistics", which are third-party startups dedicated to delivering their products.

By better understanding these drivers, you can model the effects of rising consumer demand, fees and other barriers, and the supply-side cost structures. You can then predict the likely online share in each sector under different scenarios.

For example, the U.K. has one of the world's most advanced grocery markets, but costly packaging and delivery still require fees or minimum basket sizes. It is likely, if current fee levels persist in the U.K., that the online share of food retail will probably peak at 8 percent, not far above the current level of 6 percent. However, if costs decline and fees disappear, online share could rise to 16 percent by 2030.

Furthermore, the impact of COVID-19 on food delivery has been huge in the short term. The longer-term implications at this point aren't yet clear but it has certainly given a lot of good exposure to the general population who in the past would have never considered home delivery or curbside pickup.

In order to reduce last-mile delivery costs and keep your customers happy, start thinking less about expenses, and more about improving efficiency, from the moment the order is placed until it's delivered. Efficient, cost-effective delivery operations will only improve the customer experience, whether their journey starts in brick-and-mortar retail stores or online [Oliver Wyman, 2018].

Three Steps for Reducing Last-Mile Delivery Costs

Some ways to reduce last-mile delivery costs are:

1. Implement better order batching and routing – Efficiently handling a greater number of SKUs requires automated order fulfillment. The same logic applies to automated dispatching and routing for deliveries that are planned in advance.
2. Offer more flexible delivery options – Having more delivery options can actually reduce delivery costs. When companies provide their customers with flexible delivery options, quite a few will choose an option that is less expensive for the business, if it's also properly incentivized for the customer by ensuring better delivery fulfillment that addresses each customer's needs.
3. Invest in the customer experience – Investing in customer-facing communications tools and visibility will actually lower your last-mile delivery costs by reducing failed deliveries [Bringg, 2019].

Partnerships Save Time and Money

Many retailers have found it difficult to deliver improvements in online shopping. Some of the new capabilities are costly to develop and often require the right skills. They also face a higher cost of capital than online incumbents and startups and often fear that their efforts in online retail could take away from brick-and-mortar operations.

As we have discussed previously in this book, there is always the option to obtain the necessary capabilities elsewhere. Traditionally, retailers have used their own trucks for home deliveries, but from now on, someone else might fulfill the task (e.g. DHL delivers for Amazon Fresh in Germany).

A greater variety of services is likely to come along such as passive-cooling packaging where non-refrigerated vehicles can be used, which might allow Uber Eats-type arrangements to emerge. To enhance the shopping experience, Walmart has partnered with Google Home to deliver a seamless voice-ordering experience.

This isn't just for the "big guys", as retailers of all sizes are adopting the tactic. For example, smaller supermarkets such as Morrisons are turning to Ocado, an online supermarket with no stores of its own, and Primark, GNC, and Trader Joe's are partnering with e-commerce platform specialists such as Aptos.

Omni-channel will grow with changes in attitudes and technical literacy, but also because of barrier removal as innovations make e-commerce more efficient and more fun [Oliver Wyman, 2018].

GENERATIONAL INFLUENCE

The ability to touch and try on a product before purchase is less and less of a concern for Generation Z (born 1997–2012), the new segment for rising brands and apps to capture loyalty, than it has been for Baby Boomers (born 1946–1964), Generation X (born 1965–1980), or even Millennials (born 1981–1996). Instead, brand coverage, social media presence, and overall lifestyle preference sells Gen Z on their one-click purchase on Amazon or through the newest app as well as influencing how older generations shop, too.

In general, Gen Z is very comfortable with e-commerce (only 9.6 percent report buying items in a physical store) by engaging with more ads, buying on newer platforms, spending more discretionary income, and spending two to three times more shopping on social channels than the average consumer, largely with Instagram and Snapchat shopping. Gen X tends to prefer Facebook shopping.

One thing they all have in common today is that nobody shops exclusively through a single medium. Consumers of all generations buy online, in store, and on marketplaces.

Only 13 percent of consumers believe companies are reaching this potential and delivering on multiple platforms, despite the fact that more and more studies show how important customer experience is. So omni-channel marketing is an opportunity that retailers and brands need to expand upon [Wallace, 2020].

To support this thesis, research by the Chief Marketing Officer (CMO) Council in partnership with Pitney Bowes found that despite generational differences:

- Coverage across the various channels is an expected standard which 91 percent of consumers believed was critical.
- Intimacy and trust between the brand and consumer are important across all generations.
- There is an expectation for brands to remember their consumers in the transition between channels.

The amount of data and the technologies available today make this a feasible goal, but ultimately, it's the brands that implement these capabilities that will be the leaders in the future [Dua, 2019].

OMNI-CHANNEL ECOSYSTEM

When retailers moved from multi-channel retail to a more integrated omni-channel approach, they created a smooth and efficient shopping experience for their customers. The next stage of the journey is to evolve from omni-channel retail to a fully functioning, integrated omni-channel retail "ecosystem".

This ecosystem will allow retailers to use networks of partners, vendors, and digital services to provide shoppers with a completely seamless experience, giving their customers what they want. This next step in the evolution of omni-channel retail will be driven by data mining and analytics. It will provide companies with the information they need to successfully market their products and services and to provide shoppers with the smooth, integrated experience they expect.

Why Companies Should Invest in Omni-Channel Ecosystems

Adopting a fully integrated ecosystem will take the convenience and personalization of omni-channel retail even further, which should benefit the companies that go down this path.

To support this thought, research from the Harvard Business Review showed that the more touchpoints a customer uses, the more they end up spending. So, if businesses can keep customers within their ecosystem, moving from touchpoint to touchpoint, the customer's overall expenditure should tend to be higher.

The Benefits of an Omni-Channel Ecosystem

The main benefits to consumers of an omni-channel retail ecosystem are increased convenience and personalization, and for businesses, an increase in profits.

Congruent with this, omni-channel payment systems are becoming an area of interest for all businesses. An omni-channel approach provides customers with a variety of options at the checkout (besides traditional ones such as credit cards) such as PayPal, Apple Pay, Android Pay, and payment on collection. This is an important foundation concept to the successful implementation of an omni-channel ecosystem.

Factors to Consider When Developing an Omni-Channel Strategy

Individual ecosystems, while having many services in common, will need to be tailored to individual retailers implementing their own strategy with their customers. There should be a strong correlation between online and offline stores, with branding, corporate image, and level of customer service the same across all platforms.

The entire customer experience should be intuitive, effortless, and seamless, requiring significant investment in specialized IT support. Requiring customers to login to your online store helps to monitor unique shopping habits as well as the fact that when they get in touch either in store or by phone, you have all of their information at hand, enabling you to personalize their experience.

Optimizing Each Channel in an Omni-Channel Experience

Even though you'll need to look at your ecosystem as a whole to make sure that it works smoothly, it's also important to analyze each step of the process individually. Look at the ways your customers currently interact with your company, talk and engage with your customers about how you could enhance their shopping experience, and determine which elements of omni-channel retail are most important to them.

If you plan on using third parties to provide you with omni-channel services, it's important to use businesses with experience in this area to help you build your integrated omni-channel ecosystem.

By creating and implementing a complete strategy for your ecosystem, you can offer your customers an enhanced buying experience, and personalized service. As mentioned previously, omni-channel retail is increasingly popular with consumers from all demographics, so your strategy should yield greater profits, enhanced customer loyalty, and a solid online and offline presence well into the future [Card Connect, 2020].

SUPPLY CHAIN OF THE FUTURE: KEY PRINCIPLES IN BUILDING AN OMNI-CHANNEL DISTRIBUTION NETWORK

As omni-channel shopping is becoming the "go-to" strategy, companies must be prepared to support this integrated "any time, any place" approach with a different supply chain network, as discussed in Chapter 10. This is easier said than done, as it requires a very short time between order and delivery, with excellent service and accommodating convenience.

According to consultant McKinsey's white paper "Supply Chain of the Future: Key Principles in Building an Omni-Channel Distribution Network" [Fleischer, Graf and Lange, 2020], companies that succeed in omni-channel use seven key building blocks required of the omni-channel supply chain, as traditional supply chain networks typically are not designed for same-day delivery with excellent service. The building blocks (Figure 19.1) are:

1. Customer-centric supply chain strategy – This is the starting point where you need to design an omni-channel supply chain that meets customer needs in all channels.
2. Network and ecosystem of the future – This is the supply chain's backbone that provides the required speed and flexibility, while leveraging information, partner assets, and capabilities.

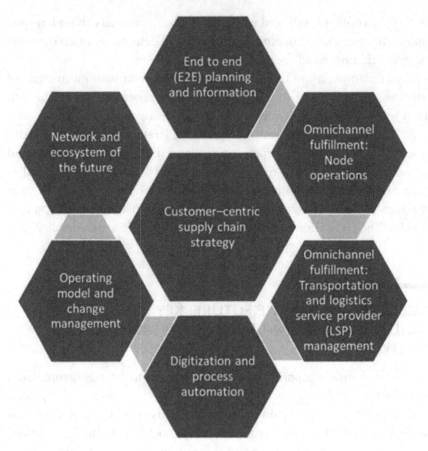

FIGURE 19.1
The seven supply chain building blocks for omni-channel excellence.

3. End-to-end (E2E) planning and information – An organization must have access to key information flow capabilities, often in real time, that are necessary to deliver according to the multitude of customer expectations.

4. Omni-channel fulfillment: Transportation and logistics service provider (LSP) management – Key physical flow resource capabilities provide reliable, fast service to all customers where it matters, while effectively managing transportation costs.

5. Omni-channel fulfillment: Node operations – Have critical physical flow capabilities in warehouse fulfillment operations with competitive cost structures and reliable quality while managing complexity.

6. Operating model and change management – A key organizational enabler for the company and its people designed to realize supply chain potential and deliver customer value.

7. Digitization and process automation – An important technology enabler that uses available omni-channel data, analytics, and supply chain systems along the end-to-end value chain, including ecosystem partners.

To accomplish this, the McKinsey white paper concludes that you should focus on the following concepts to be successful in the long term:

Put the customer's needs first – Companies need to identify, in detail, what the customer really wants. This tells them which channels to serve, which products and services to offer, and where to offer them.

Forget one size fits all – Retailers today need a deep understanding of customer desires to help create a strategy that includes the building of customer segments based on preferences, product categories, and locations.

Be fast and collaborative – In the traditional supply chain model, companies rely more on a purely quantitative, fairly static approach to model the fulfillment network needed for the service offering. In omni-channel, reacting quickly with an efficient, flexible supply chain is critical.

Seek partnerships and share resources – In today's volatile environment, speed of implementation and efficient use of resources are extremely important. So, your company should be prepared to take advantage of existing infrastructure in your ecosystem, such as warehouses and retail stores, as well as available third-party resources.

Look for innovative fulfillment options – When identifying existing assets within a company and its partners' networks, it is important to consider innovative fulfillment options throughout their ecosystem.

Think early about new capabilities and never stop learning – To enable the creative solutions that they come up with, companies must consider the capabilities required to run their future network and understand how to design and implement them.

I think this is great advice that you can truly "take to the bank".

In today's omni-channel environment, customers are the new market-makers, reshaping industries and changing how businesses compete and prosper. Success depends on how well and how fast you respond. I hope that this book has given you some insights and frameworks to shorten the time between great ideas and great results, helping your organizations to win in the age of the customer.

References

"4PL Supply Chain Transformation, Menlo Worldwide Logistics White Paper", 2014. www.con-way.com (accessed: 2014).

"7 Barriers to Perfect Omni-Channel Retail Customer Experience", *Core Management Logistics*, 2019. www.cmlplc.com (accessed: 2020).

Agrawal, A.J. "How the Digital Age Has Changed Marketing Channels Forever", *Forbes*, February 15, 2016. www.forbes.com.

Armstrong & Associates, Inc. "Ryder Supply Chain Solutions Site Visits –3PL Case Study Reports, 2007 and 2013". www.3plogistics.com (accessed: 2014).

Armstrong, Gary and Kotler, Philip *Marketing*, 13th Edition. Pearson, 2017, pp. 24–28.

Berman, Barry and Evans, Joel R. *Retail Management: A Strategic Approach*, 12th Edition. Pearson, 2012, pp. 23–24.

Beron, Russell "6 Amazing Statistics: The Effect ECommerce Has on Supply Chains and Global Retail Sourcing", June 19, 2018. www.cbxsoftware.com (accessed: 2019).

Bringg Team "How to Cut Last Mile Delivery Costs: 3 Strategic Solutions", Bringg, March 11, 2019. www.bringg.com (accessed: 2020).

Bullard, Brittany "What is Omnichannel Analytics? Smart Retailers Know it's not Just about Marketing Anymore", SAS Insights. www.sas.com (accessed: 2020).

CB Insights "We Analyzed 14 of the Biggest Direct-to-Consumer Success Stories to Figure Out the Secrets to Their Growth — Here's What We Learned", September 19, 2019. www.cbinsights.com (accessed: 2020).

Christopher, Martin and Peck, Helen "Building the Resilient Supply Chain", Cranfield School of Management, *International Journal of Logistics Management*, 15(2), 1–13, 2004.

Copeland, Michael V. "Death by a Billion Clicks", *Wired Magazine*, November 16, 2012. www.wired.com (accessed: 2019).

"CRM", Salesforce Learning Center, salesforce.com. https://www.salesforce.com/eu/learning-centre/crm/ (accessed: 2018).

Deyo, Kristen "4 Ways to Power the Omnichannel Retail Experience with Artificial Intelligence", Orchestra CMS. www.orchestracms.com (accessed: 2020).

Dimov, Charles "What Exactly is Omni-Channel Fulfillment?", *Order Dynamics*, August 28, 2018. www.orderdynamics.com (accessed: 2019).

Dua, Taylor "Omnichannel is Best Suited for All Generations, CMO Council Study Says", *The Drum*, July 25, 2019. www.thedrum.com (accessed: 2020).

"Enhance Omnichannel Visibility - How to Gain Visibility Across the Extended Supply Chain", GTNEXUS, an Infor Company. A Strategic Imperative for Retailers White Paper, 2017.

Felker, Brent "Retail Transformation: Strategies to Make 'Fulfill from Store': A Reality", *Multi-Channel Merchant*, April 13, 2018. www.multichannelmerchant.com (accessed: 2019).

Fleischer, Wolfgang, Graf, Claudia, and Lange, Tim *Supply Chain of the Future: Key Principles in Building an Omni-Channel Distribution Network*. McKinsey & Company, 2020. www.mckinsey.com (accessed: 2020).

Gilmore, Dan "Just What is a Supply Chain Strategy?", Supply Chain Digest, October 4, 2013. www.scdigest.com (accessed: 2019).

Gonzalez, Adrian "Transportation Sourcing in an Omni-Channel World", *Talking Logistics*, April 29, 2015. www.talkinglogistics.com (accessed: 2019).

Greaver, Maurice F. "Strategic Outsourcing", AMACOM (an imprint of American Management Association publications), 1999. www.asaecenter.org (accessed: 2014).

Hanks, Jeremy "Evolving the Supply Chain in the Ecommerce Age", *Multi-Channel Merchant*, August 12, 2013. www.multichannelmerchant.com (accessed: 2018).

Heizer, Jay and Render, Barry *Operations Management*, 11th Edition. Pearson, 2013, p. 438.

Hitachi Consulting "Six Key Trends Changing Supply Chain Management Today – Choosing the Optimal Strategy for Your Business", *A Knowledge-Driven White Paper*, 2009.

Hogenson, Andrew "Omnichannel. It's Become the Standard Approach to Retail. The Lines between E-commerce, Physical Stores and Mobile Have so Blurred that the Consumer no Longer Makes a Distinction", March 19, 2018. www.consulting.ey.com (accessed: 2020).

Ishfaq, Rafay, Gibson, Brian J., and Defee, C. Clifford "How Retailers Are Getting Ready for an Omnichannel World", *Supply Chain Quarterly Magazine*, Quarter 2, 2016.

Kaplan, Deborah Abrams "The Real Cost of E-Commerce Logistics", *Supply Chain Drive*, June 6, 2017. www.supplychaindrive (accessed: 2019).

Kauffman, Ralph G. and Crimi, Thomas A. "A Best-Practice Approach for Development of Global Supply Chains", 90th Annual International Supply Management Conference, San Antonio, TX, May 2005.

Kourimsky, Hans and van der Berk, Marc "The Impact of Omni-Channel Commerce on Supply Chains: How to Make Sure You Effectively Deliver Products that Meet the Customer's Expectations", *White Paper*, Itelligence, 2014. www.itelligencegroup.com (accessed: 2019).

Krajewski, Lee J., Ritzman, Larry P., and Malhotra, Manoj K. *Operations Management: Processes and Supply Chains*, 10th Edition. Pearson Higher Education, 2013, pp. 11–12.

Levy, Michael and Weitz, Barton *Retail Management*, 8th Edition. McGraw-Hill Irwin, 2012, pp. 6–8.

Lim, Kenneth "5 Key Considerations for Your Reverse Supply Logistics Strategy", *Digital Flipbook Download*, October 10, 2017. www.optoro.com (accessed: 2019).

Marrs, Megan "What is Mobile Marketing & Why Does it Matter So Much?", WordStream.com, December 13, 2017.

Meyer, Bernard "How Net-A-Porter Used Omnichannel Marketing for Amazing Results (& How You Can Do the Same)", *Marketing Tips*, May 24, 2018. www.omnisend.com (accessed: 2018).

Miller, Davis "The Role of the Internet in Supply Chain Management", February 26, 2013. www.grahamjones.co.uk (accessed: 2018).

Myerson, Paul *Lean Supply Chain & Logistics Management*. McGraw-Hill Professional, 2012, pp. 11–16.

Myerson, Paul "A Lean and Agile Supply Chain: Not an Option, But a Necessity", *Inbound Logistics Magazine*, October 16, 2014.

Myerson, Paul A. "Distribution Disruption: Ready or Not, Here It Comes", *Industry Week Magazine*, May 6, 2016a.

Myerson, Paul A. "E-Commerce is Driving the Industrial Real Estate Market", *Industry Week Magazine*, September 30, 2016b.

Myerson, Paul A. "How Supply Chain Strategies Impact E-commerce Success", *Inbound Logistics Magazine*, November 14, 2016c.

Myerson, Paul A. "Omnichannel Multiplies the Challenges for Distribution-Centric Supply Chains", *Industry Week Magazine*, June 1, 2018a. www.industryweek.com.

Myerson, Paul A. "Are You Ready for Omnichannel Retail?", *Inbound Logistics Magazine*, July 16, 2018b.

Myerson, Paul A. "Retailers Seek to Tweak the Last Mile", *Industry Week Magazine*, August 19, 2018c.

Myerson, Paul A. "Store Delivery Keeps Retailers in the Game", *Inbound Logistics Magazine*, September 14, 2018d.

Myerson, Paul A. "Riding Out the Rapids", *Inbound Logistics Magazine*, January 31, 2019a.

Myerson, Paul A. "Omnichannel Retail: 4 Rules for Success", *Inbound Logistics Magazine*, March 4, 2019b.

Myerson, Paul A. "Managing Change in Turbulent Times", *Inbound Logistics Magazine*, May 31, 2019c.

Myerson, Paul A. "The Road Map Out of This Mess", *Inbound Logistics Magazine*, May 2020.

"Navigating the Future of Omnichannel Retailing", Card Connect. www.cardconnect. com (accessed: 2020).

"Omnichannel is Dead; Long Live the Omnichannel", abolutdata.com, January 20, 2015. www.absolutdata.com (accessed: 2020).

"Omni-Channel Retail, A Deloitte Point of View", Deloitte, 2015. www2.deloitte.com.

"Operations & Fulfillment: 5 Steps to Omnichannel Success", July 1, 2013. www.mytotal-retail.com (accessed: 2019).

Porter, Michael *Competitive Advantage: Creating and Sustaining Superior Performance.* Free Press, 1998.

PwC and the MIT Forum for Supply Chain Innovation "Making the Right Risk Decisions to Strengthen Operations Performance", 2013. www.pwc.com (accessed: 2014).

"Re-engineering the Supply Chain for the Omni-Channel of Tomorrow - Global Consumer Goods and Retail Omni-Channel Supply Chain Survey", EY and the Consumer Goods Forum Supply Chain Committee, February 2015a. www.ey.com (accessed: 2019).

"Re-engineering the Supply Chain for the Omni-Channel of Tomorrow", EY in Collaboration with the CGF: Re-engineering the Supply Chain for the Omni-Channel of Tomorrow, September 2015b. www.ey.com (accessed: 2019).

Reiser, Clint "E-commerce and the Warehouse of Tomorrow", June 13, 2016. www. dcvelocity.com (accessed: 2019).

Reverse Logistics Magazine Staff Contributor "Best Buy Turning Returns Processing into Profit Center", *Reverse Logistics Magazine*, Edition 15, January 2009. www. reverselogsticstrends.com (accessed: 2014).

Rikhy, Swecha "5 Ways to an Agile Supply Chain: Winning the Omni-Channel Race", *Tata Consultancy Services Corporate Themes*, April 7, 2016. www.tcs.com (accessed: 2019).

Robinson, Nick "Omnichannel Urgency: Retail at the Customer Experience Tipping Point", April 22, 2014. www.supplychain247.com (accessed: 2018).

Rosing, Jason "Differences between Omnichannel & Omnichannel 2.0", *Supply Chain News*, January 14, 2019. www.supplychain247.com (accessed: 2019).

Saddle Creek Logistics Services "Optimizing Omnichannel Distribution through Outsourcing", White Paper, 2016. www.sclogistics.com (accessed: 2019).

SCDigest Editorial Staff "The Five Challenges of Today's Global Supply Chains", August 12, 2010. www.scdigest.com (accessed: 2014).

Sheffield, Yossi and Rice Jr., James B. "A Supply Chain View of the Resilient Enterprise", *MIT Sloan Management Review*, 47(1), 41–48, Fall 2005.

Smyyth LLC "History of Retailing in North America", 2011. www.smyyth.com (accessed: 2018).

"Social Media Marketing for Businesses", WordStream. www.wordstream.com (accessed: 2018).

Staff "The Customer Journey Mindset: Your Key to Success in an Omni-Channel World", Three Deep Marketing, September 23, 2019.

"The Future of Retail is Omnichannel", Oliver Wyman, 2018. www.oliverwyman.com (accessed: 2020).

"The Single View of the Customer", September 28, 2018. www.evolveip.com (accessed: 2020).

Thomas, Kelly "Supply Chain Segmentation: 10 Steps to Greater Profits", *CSCMP Supply Chain Quarterly*, Quarter 1, 2012.

Thompson, Scott "Analysis: Walmart Accelerates Omnichannel Innovation", Essential Retail, February 2018. www.essentialretail.com (accessed: 2019).

"Top of Mind – Issues Facing Technology Companies - Supply Chain Segmentation", Ernst & Young. www.ey.com (accessed: 2014).

Trout, Jason "5 Excellent Examples of Omnichannel Retailing Done Right", February 2, 2017. www.multichannelmerchant.com (accessed: 2018).

Waldron, John "How Home Depot Nails Omnichannel Supply Chain Fulfillment", 2019. www.etaileast.com (accessed: 2019).

Wallace, Tracey "Omni-Channel Retail Report: Generational Consumer Shopping Behavior Comes into Focus + Its Importance in Ecommerce", Big Commerce, 2020. www.bigcommerce.com (accessed: 2020).

"What is Going on in Last Mile Delivery, Omnichannel Retail and Transportation and Logistics? 2019 Trends in Last Mile Delivery, Omnichannel Retail, Transportation and Logistics", Update on the Latest Trends in Omnichannel Retail: Part 1, 2019. www.datexcorp.com (accessed: 2019).

Young, Jessica "US Commerce Sales Grow 14.9% in 2019", Digital Commerce 360, February 19, 2020. www.digitalcommerce360.com (accessed: 2020).

Ziegler, Maxwell "3 Challenges of Omni-Channel Order Fulfillment", October 1, 2018. www.conveyco.com (accessed: 2019).

Index

Printed in the United States
By Bookmasters